WILD PLACES
OF THE SOUTH

Steve Price

The
East Woods
Press

* Library of Congress Cataloging in Publication Data

Price, Steve, 1947 —
  Wild places of the South.

  Includes index.
  1. Wilderness areas — Southern States — Guide-books.
  2. Southern States — Description and travel — Guide books.
  I. Title.
  QH76.5.S69P74   917.5′ 04′ 4   79-26290
  ISBN 0-914788-22-1

Photographs by Steve Price unless otherwise indicated.
Typography by Raven.
Printed in the United States of America
  by Hunter Publishing Company.

East Woods Press Books
Fast & McMillan Publishers
820 East Boulevard
Charlotte, NC 28203

ABOUT THE AUTHOR

Steve Price's writing reflects his commitment to the preservation and celebration of this nation's wilderness. A former U.S. Army photo officer, he has traveled widely throughout the world as a writer, photographer and outdoor recreation specialist.

The former outdoor editor of SOUTHERN LIVING, Steve has contributed numerous articles to many outdoor magazines, among them FIELD & STREAM, OUTDOOR LIFE, SPORTS AFIELD, FISHING WORLD and SALT WATER SPORTSMAN. He is the author of WORLD CHAMPIONSHIP BASS FISHING.

Steve lives with his wife Betty and their daughter in Birmingham, Alabama where he devotes his full time to free-lance work.

ACKNOWLEDGEMENTS

A book of this type takes the combined efforts of many people whose help was essential to this project. In this case, I would like to express my sincere appreciation to the many members of both the U.S. Forest Service and National Park Service who patiently answered my thousands of questions, helped in trip planning and often acted as personal guides.

A special thanks goes to Dr. Charles Fryling of Baton Rouge for introducing the wonders of the Atchafalaya Basin; to Bob McDaniel and Rudy Mancke for showing me the forest giants of Congaree Swamp; to Paul McCrary and Jackie Kolk for an enchanting tour of Cumberland Island; to Ralph Kiel and Kriste Steinhauer who helped unlock the mysteries of Great Dismal Swamp; and to Barney Cone, former U.S. Fish and Wildlife Service agent, for an absolutely unforgettable trip through the Okefenokee.

Russ Daley, Information Officer for the U.S. Forest Service Southern Region, also deserves a nod of appreciation for his help in providing valuable background information on many of the wild places included in this book.

Last but not least, I am grateful to my wife Betty, a wonderful wilderness companion who has packed and paddled and explored the wild places with me on three continents.

CONTENTS

INTRODUCTION

The last two decades in America have seen incredible advances in all phases of technology, advancements that would have seemed impossible just half a century ago. Scientists are sending space ships to Jupiter, Saturn and the planets beyond; chemists are developing synthetic fuels to heat homes and power automobiles; doctors are completely wiping out diseases that once claimed thousands of lives annually.

Along with these advances, an increasing awareness of the outdoor world has also taken hold. People are flocking to the mountains, the rivers, the seashores and the forests in ever-growing numbers, for man has learned he must periodically escape his own technology in order to better understand it. And with each subsequent "escape," the meaning of Thoreau's famous words becomes more and more clear: "In wildness is the preservation of the world."

It is easy to reaffirm the magnificence of the natural world when you can fill your canteen from a cascading stream, look out from the ridge of a mountain and see mile after mile of rolling forest or watch in quiet wonder as a mother bear teaches two young cubs to dig grubs from a fallen log. With experiences such as these has also come a commitment to preserve and protect the wild places that technology has not reached. In the South and East, most of the wilderness areas are reclaimed tracts in which timber had been harvested, wildlife eliminated and streams polluted. But today these are the very places where it is possible to fill your canteen, or watch the mother bear with her cubs.

That is good, because it means preservation is possible.

This book is not written to act as an actual trail or river guide to the wild places listed. Instead, its purpose is to inform you that such places exist, and to encourage you to visit them and help preserve them.

There are many, many more wild places in the South besides just these. West Virginia's New River is rugged and challenging as it churns through a deep canyon; Florida's Bradwell Bay Wilderness is a hardwood swamp filled with a variety of wildlife; and portions of Gulf Islands National Seashore are as secluded and isolated as any island in the South Pacific.

So shoulder your pack and hit the trail! The outdoor world is waiting for your discovery.

HOW TO PLAN YOUR WILDERNESS TRIP

The key to enjoying any wilderness area is prior planning. Even the day-use areas will be more enjoyable if you read some of the region's history, learn what species of wildlife might be seen and know exactly what kind of terrain you will encounter. It is one thing to start out the morning on a fairly level, well-traveled trail heading through the trees, but quite another to discover that trail is impassable two miles ahead due to high water.

Planning is more critical for long-distance trips. While no Southern wilderness is very far from civilization, in times of emergency the shortest distance can be too far. You cannot prepare for *every* emergency that may befall you and your companions in the backcountry, but you can be ready for most of them.

The first step in planning any trip is to contact the agency in charge of the wilderness you plan to visit and request any maps or brochures describing the area. In most cases this material will be free of charge and will include enough information for you to decide if indeed you do want to visit the region. If, after reading and studying this information, you still have questions, telephone or write the agency again. You will find members of the National Park Service, U.S. Forest Service, Fish and Wildlife Service and other administrative organizations extremely helpful and cooperative.

If backpacking is involved, you may want to purchase a topographic map of the area which will show the elevation changes as well as locations of rivers, roads and trails. In many wilderness areas trail systems have been designed to interconnect and allow numerous trip variations. Topo maps are usually available from the administration headquarters office of the wilderness you plan to visit and are quite inexpensive.

Initial information on the wilderness you plan to visit should also include the various rules and regulations in effect for that area. Firearms, fireworks and alcoholic beverages are normally prohibited; dogs must be kept on leash (if permitted at all); and camping may be restricted to certain areas due to fire hazards, human impact or site maintenance.

The ideal time to visit any wilderness area is whenever you can. For the majority of people today, this means during a weekend or holiday. If the wilderness area you choose to visit requires a use permit, apply for it early in case permit limits are in effect. If you plan to fish or hunt, make certain you obtain the proper licenses and are familiar with various state regulations.

All the wild places in this book can be seen only on foot or by boat, usually canoe. Many of the hiking trails are steep and the rivers require hard or extended paddling. It is really important to be physically fit to meet these conditions, not only for yourself but for the others with you. Backpacking does not require the stamina demanded of Olympic marathoners, but it will certainly be more enjoyable when leg muscles are not strained at every step. If you know you are heading into particularly rugged country, a conditioning program of exercising and jogging will ease the burden of carrying a pack immeasurably. Short after-dinner walks through your neighborhood will aid in conditioning office-bound muscles.

During these afternoon walks, you may want to wear your hiking boots or even carry a pack. Do not worry about what the neighbors will say; most will be envious when you tell them of your upcoming trek into the north Georgia mountains or through the West Virginia evergreen forests. If your boots are well worn, you will benefit by getting your feet accustomed to them. If you footwear is new, wearing them a little now will soften the leather and prevent blisters and possible sprains later.

Do not attempt to make one of the canoeing trips described in this book without first obtaining some paddling instruction. It is a fairly simple matter to keep a canoe headed in a straight line in flat water once the proper technique is learned, but it is an altogether different ball game in foaming white water. Throughout the Southeast there are numerous organizations and outfitters that can provide proper instruction in canoeing, and most furnish all the necessary equipment. Check with your

local outdoor/camping supply shop for the names of outfitters in your area.

There is no question that having the proper equipment can make any outdoor experience better. Today's packs distribute weights over the shoulders and hips better than ever, so that the term "human pack mule" is no longer valid. Tents are not only stronger and roomier, but lighter as well. In backpacking equipment, any two-person tent weighing more than five pounds is heavy. Modern sleeping bags that will keep a person warm in subzero temperatures weigh less than three pounds.

The wilderness experience still has room for the evening campfire too, but most of today's serious campers prefer to use small portable stoves. There are many different models on the market, most of them easy to operate, quite efficient and able to function on either propane, butane, alcohol or unleaded gas.

If you purchase any new equipment such as a stove or a new tent, make sure you know how to operate it before heading into a wilderness area. Pitch your tent in the yard and light the stove a couple of times just to make sure all the poles are included and that the stove does not leak.

Do not neglect food. Contrary to what your boots may tell you, a backpacker travels on his stomach, not his feet. Hiking and canoeing are both high-energy activities that burn up a lot of calories. Proper food is critical to the enjoyment of either sport. Today's freeze-dried food, available in most camping/ trail shops, is extremely lightweight as well as expensive. It also takes water, which may or may not be readily available. You may decide these foods are just what you require, or you may want to supplement them with regular items from your grocery store.

Many store-bought "instant" foods are actually faster to prepare than some freeze-dried items, and when properly packaged can be just as light. Half the fun in preparing for a backpacking or canoeing trip is trying to cut down excess weight and size, and repackaging specific food portions in plastic bags or wrapping in aluminum foil will certainly cut ounces off your load.

Last but not least, do not leave all your packing to the last minute—that's the time you discover the coffee pot has a broken handle, the tent pole is bent or your flashlight needs new batteries. Make a list of the items you plan to take and gradually assemble them over a period of a week or more.

The gold, they say, is in the going, but the experience will be that much more golden if you plan it right.

WILD PLACES OF THE SOUTH

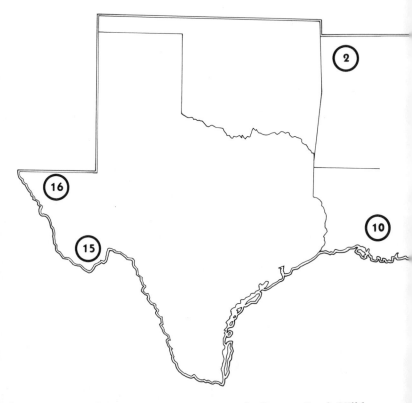

1. Sipsey Wilderness
2. The Caney Creek Wilderness
3. The Wilderness Waterway
4. The Chattooga River
5. The Cohutta Wilderness
6. Okefenokee Swamp
7. Cumberland Island
8. Cumberland Gap
   National Historic Park

9. Beaver Creek Wilderness
10. Atchafalaya Basin
11. Linville Gorge Wilderness
12. Shining Rock Wilderness
13. Joyce Kilmer Wilderness
14. Congaree Swamp
15. Big Bend Canyons
16. Guadalupe Mountains

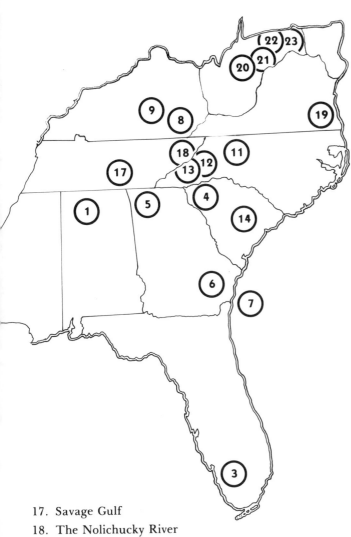

ALABAMA

From its northern mountains to southern coast, Alabama can provide a variety of outdoor experiences, although there is only one congressionally-designated wilderness area, Sipsey. Hiking and canoeing are quite popular.

The Alabama Conservancy, based in Birmingham, has been quite active in promoting the preservation of wild places and often sponsors hikes, canoe trips and overnight outings to various locales in an effort to better inform the public.

The state is generally rural, but highways are good through most counties. The major cities are Birmingham, Montgomery and Mobile, and most air traffic in Alabama eventually funnels through one of them. A number of outdoor shops specializing in backpacking, camping, and canoeing equipment are located in the major cities. Most will rent equipment.

Fall is generally the best season for an outing, for then the mosquitos, heat and humidity have largely disappeared. Some snow usually falls in the northern portion of the state in late winter, but seldom remains long on the ground. Wildlife, especially deer and turkey, is abundant, and hunting seasons are generous, so fall hikers should be especially cautious when traveling in hunting areas.

ALABAMA'S SIPSEY WILDERNESS
"A Scenic Walk to Bee Branch"

They say that if you sit quietly by your evening campfire beneath the big popular tree in Bee Branch, you can still hear the voices of the Creeks, Cherokees and Chickasaws who once roamed these Alabama woodlands. They may be talking about one of the chieftans they left behind, buried in a sitting position at the mouth of a cave overlooking Borden Creek. This creek is just one of dozens of streams lacing through northern Alabama's Bankhead National Forest, and because it is rugged canyon country, there are numerous caves along most of the waterways. No one has ever found the chieftan, although many have searched.

The Indian tribes believed this region of clear-flowing streams, abundant wildlife and cool summer breezes to be healthful, as did pioneering settlers behind them. One of the most refreshing spots is Bee Branch Scenic Area, located in the 12,000-acre Sipsey Wilderness, a few miles north of Borden Creek.

Bee Branch is a steep-walled box canyon, filled with moss-covered boulders and thriving hardwoods. The Alabama State Champion Yellow Poplar grows at the head of this narrow gorge, fed by a clear stream splashing in from the cliffs above. Reaching the quiet restfulness of Bee Branch is like receiving a present from Mother Nature after enduring the hike in.

Geographically, this region is located at the junction of the Appalachian Plateau, the Cumberland Plateau and the Gulf Coastal Plain, and contains a mixture of each. Along with the hardwoods there are wild azaleas, colorful orchids and places where the soil is as sandy as any ocean beach.

The Alabama Champion Yellow Poplar is a massive tree growing in Bee Branch among the mossy rocks. It is easily recognizable, for no other nearby trees are as large.

The trail leading to this canyon is not strenuous and measures only about a mile in length. It appears more like an old logging road, although this part of the forest has reportedly never been cut. There is a mixture of oak, hickory, holly and dogwood, and some of the trees are extremely large. Deer are common in this part of the state and are often seen by hikers who leave the main trail.

Much of the Sipsey Wilderness is characterized by the same type of terrain as Bee Branch: steep, rugged canyons heavily forested with pine or second-growth hardwoods. The streams are clear and cold when there is water in them, a fact the area's first explorer, Hernando De Soto, reported during his travels in 1540. He described "bad passages and cold rivers."

Camping on the floor of the narrow canyon is not encouraged. Although Bee Branch may be dry in the summer months, it does get wet and even floods during heavy rains. Forest Service officials in Double Springs prefer that visitors avoid the area if flooding is a possibility.

Sipsey receives heavy use, however, at all times of the year. It is scenic, a little bit of solitude tucked away from nearby cities — and at the present time, it is Alabama's only congressionally-recognized wilderness.

HOW TO VISIT THE SIPSEY WILDERNESS

This 12,000-acre wilderness, created by Congress in 1975, is extremely easy to locate and, as a result, sees heavy use. It is approximately a two-hour drive northwest of Birmingham, in the rolling hills of the Bankhead National Forest.

To reach the Sipsey Wilderness and Bee Branch Scenic Area, follow U.S. Highway 278 west from Cullman approximately 45 miles to Double Springs. Turn north in Double Springs on Ala. Highway 33, and follow this road about 9 miles to County Road 60, which leads to the Sipsey River Recreation Area. Turn west on County Road 60, and after 0.5-mile turn right on unpaved Forest Service Road 224. Follow this gravel road 6.5 miles to an obvious parking pullout on the left, the trailhead for the path leading to Bee Branch.

HIKING AND BACKPACKING: Both day hiking and backpacking are popular in the Sipsey, with the most popular route being the Bee Branch Trail, leading from FS 224 to Bee Branch and its accompanying virgin hardwoods. This mile-

22

long trail is easy to follow and is not steep until the last 100-yard descent into a rocky box canyon.

Other recognized hiking trails in this part of the national forest include walking paths at Sipsey River and Natural Bridge recreation areas, but both are extremely short. Intrepid backpackers can explore the dense hardwood forest and rocky gorges of the region on their own with little trouble or follow the numerous logging roads.

CAMPING: Camping is permitted anywhere in the Sipsey, and evidence of past campsites can be seen on the Bee Branch Trail and in the canyon. The best primitive camping is along the relatively level trail leading into Bee Branch, for the canyon is filled with huge boulders and trees. If you do not mind sleeping under big rocks, there are several in the canyon that offer some shelter from rain and wind. You will have to pack in and pack out everything you use here.

Established campgrounds providing easy access to the wilderness are Brushy Lake and Corinth, which have facilities for camping trailers. Campers will enjoy swimming, boating and fishing on 33-acre Brushy Lake; at Corinth users can swim, fish and go boating on 21,000-acre Lewis Smith Lake.

FISHING AND HUNTING: Fishing is good for largemouth and spotted bass and various species of bream in Lewis Smith Lake, where several world-record spotted bass have been caught. Bass and bream fishing is also good during the spring in the Sipsey River when water levels are high enough for float-fishing.

Hunters can go after deer, turkey, squirrel and other game animals throughout the wilderness, which is contained within the Black Warrior Wildlife Management Area. Some of the state's largest deer are taken annually here in Winston and Lawrence counties.

For additional information, contact the Department of Conservation and National Resources, 64 N. Union Street, Montgomery, AL 36130.

WILDLIFE OBSERVATION: Quiet hikers might see deer or possibly call in a wild turkey on the hardwood ridges, but because the area is well traveled, wildlife may appear scarce. Birders may enjoy searching for hawks floating over the ridges, or slipping quietly through the trees watching for warblers, a wood thrush or other woodland species.

Along FS 224 leading to the Bee Branch trailhead the state has constructed several special food plots for the enhancement of wildlife. These places are identified with signs and are good places to watch for deer or turkey.

BOATING AND CANOEING: Boating is extremely popular on Lewis Smith Lake, located just south of the national forest, with numerous marinas and launching ramps on its shoreline.

Float-tripping is popular in the spring on the Sipsey River between the Sipsey River Recreation Area on County Road 60 and Ala. 33, a trip of less than 15 miles. There is rarely enough water in the river during the summer months for floating.

ADDITIONAL INFORMATION: For additional information, contact the Supervisor, Bankhead National Forest, P.O. Box 40, Montgomery, AL 36101; or the District Ranger, Bankhead National Forest, Double Springs, AL 35553.

Wildlife is plentiful in the area and includes deer and turkey. This baby great horned owl is one of numerous bird species found in the Sipsey.

ARKANSAS

Arkansas hikers and paddlers have two mountain ranges, 18 million acres of national forest land, and numerous mountain streams to test their skills. The designated wilderness areas and scenic rivers are Caney Creek Wilderness in the Ouachita National Forest, and the Upper Buffalo Wilderness of the Buffalo River in the Ozarks.

Looking at the Ozarks and Ouachitas it is sometimes difficult to believe this land was underwater 500 million years ago. Even before that, however, nature had begun molding the Arkansas landscape. Volcanic outbursts about 1.5 *billion* years ago uplifted these mountains several times. The sedimentary rocks formed as the area was underwater were quickly cut through by later runoff rivers, producing the terrain present today. Evidence of man in the state dates back 9000 years.

Outdoor recreation plays a major role in the state, with the cities of Little Rock, Hot Springs, Heber Springs and Mountain Home the major gateways to recreation areas. Outdoor recreational shops stock large supplies of pack and paddle gear.

Arkansas weather can be delightfully cool in summer, bitterly cold in winter, incredibly wet in spring. The best time for outdoor activities are anytime, however, for the weather can change quite rapidly here.

Wildlife is abundant, with a frequent mixing of eastern and western species.

THE CANEY CREEK WILDERNESS
"Walking through the Ouachitas"

The Caney Creek Wilderness, a 14,433-acre parcel in the heart of the rugged Ouachita National Forest of southwest Arkansas, was set aside in 1975 to preserve a segment of one of America's most unusual mountain ranges. The Ouachitas, in contrast to most of America's mountains, run east-west rather than north-south, creating some unusual ecological mixtures.

The forests of the Ouachitas are primarily oak and hickory hardwoods, with beech, maple and walnut also common. Some of these trees grow to huge sizes, but along the summit ridges of the Ouchitas all the trees are dwarfed. Winter's moist southerly winds change to fog, mist, rain and ice storms as they move up the mountainsides, with the summit trees the hardest hit. Trees get smaller and smaller the higher one climbs.

Another noticeable feature of the Ouachitas are the rock glaciers, long boulder fields moving slowly down the mountainsides like ice glaciers. The rocks do not slide and roll over each other, but slip down from the force of gravity as a continuous stream.

The Ouachitas range in elevation from 500 to about 3000 feet, but without the abrupt cliff faces and precipitous drops more common in the Ozarks further north. These mountains are primarily shale and sandstone, created by sediments of the Paleozoic era, long before dinosaurs walked the earth.

More than 1.5 million acres of these mountains are embraced in the Ouachita National Forest, and the Caney Creek Wilderness provides an undisturbed glimpse of them. The best way to see the wilderness is by hiking the nine-mile Caney Creek Trail, traversing the area from east to west, following below the lofty ridge line of Porter Mountain and skirting Caney Creek for much of the distance. This trail is generally well worn by backpacking activity so newcomers do not have trouble following it, but the numerous creek crossings present a different kind of problem, especially if the water is high. At the western trailhead, the Cossatot River must also be waded.

In dry weather with low water levels, water at the designated crossings is seldom more than 12 inches deep, but a careful examination of stream bank trees will show that floods may raise the water several feet. This trail is definitely not a place to be in time of high water.

The trail begins with a short climb, then drops down between the steep bluffs to pick up the creek, following the base of Katy Mountain to the north. Gradually this north bank drops and the south bank, the base of Porter Mountain, begins to rise more steeply. The trail eventually leaves Caney Creek and turns northward along a tributary stream, then branches back westward to the Cossatot in numerous switchbacks and short climbs.

With close proximity to the major cities of Arkansas and a reputation as some of Mid-America's most scenic regions, the Ouachita National Forest and the Caney Creek Wilderness receive heavy use. Campsites in the wilderness show definite signs of prior visitation, and care should be taken by hikers and backpackers to carry out all trash.

The trail can be hiked in either direction, but many prefer to hike from west to east, leaving their vehicles parked at Bard Springs or Shady Lake recreation areas. Vehicle parking is also permitted on Forest Service Road 31 along the western edge of the wilderness.

HOW TO VISIT CANEY CREEK WILDERNESS

Caney Creek Wilderness is located within the Ouachita National Forest, approximately 15 miles south of Mena. The area is easily reached by traveling Ark. Highway 8 southeast out of Mena, then turning south on Ark. 375. Follow this road approximately 12 miles to the junction of FS 31 and 25. Turning south on FS 31 will take you along the western boundary of the wilderness. Continuing on FS 25 eastward approximately 9 miles will lead to the intersection of FS 38, which marks the eastern boundary of the wilderness.

No motorized vehicles are allowed within the wilderness, so plan to walk. Horses are allowed.

HIKING AND BACKPACKING: Backpacking is one of the primary attractions of the Caney Creek Wilderness, and one major trail, the Caney Creek Trail, offers excellent back-country hiking and camping opportunities.

The Caney Creek Trail leads approximately nine miles through the heart of the wilderness, following and often crossing Caney Creek for much of its distance. Trailheads are located on both FS 31 and 38. Another established trail in the wilderness area is the Shady Lake Trail, which makes a one-mile loop around Shady Lake south of the wilderness area, then continues northward two more miles to the Tall Peak Fire Tower atop Porter Mountain, one of the highest points in the wilderness.

The only other established trail here is the Buckeye Mountain Trail, 0.2 mile long, leading to the summit of Buckeye Mountain. The trailhead is located on FS 38.

CAMPING: Primitive camping is permitted throughout the wilderness area. Campfires are allowed, but portable stoves are recommended. Campers should plan to purify their drinking water from the area's streams; during dry periods, campers may decide to pack their own water. Campers and hikers should also carry rain gear and a snakebite kit.

Two established campgrounds are located along the eastern boundary of the wilderness, Shady Lake and Bard Springs. Both provide sanitary facilities, picnic shelters and sites for camping trailers.

FISHING AND HUNTING: Both fishing and hunting are permitted. The wilderness is part of the 100,000-acre Caney Creek Wildlife Management Unit, administered by the Arkansas Game and Fish Commission.

Fishing is good in area streams for smallmouth bass, spotted bass and various sunfish. In addition, popular Lake Ouachita, located approximately 20 miles east of the wilderness, provides excellent bass fishing.

Hunting seasons are open for deer, turkey, bear and squirrel. For complete information on seasons and limits, write the Arkansas Game and Fish Commission, No. 2 Natural

Resources Drive, Little Rock, AR 72205.

WILDLIFE OBSERVATION: Backpackers might expect to see whitetail deer and possibly wild turkey during their hikes in the Caney Creek Wilderness. Bear are present in the region, but are seldom encountered. Smaller game, including squirrel, rabbit and raccoon, may also be seen. Bird life includes several species of hawks, numerous woodland varieties in the forests and, in winter, waterfowl on the lakes. Golden eagles are occasionally seen riding the rising air currents in the fall.

ADDITIONAL INFORMATION: Complete information about the Caney Creek Wilderness is available from the Forest Supervisor, Ouachita National Forest, Hot Springs, AR 71901; or from the District Ranger, 511 Mena Street, Mena, AR 71953. Wilderness maps are available for $.50.

The major trail of the Caney Creek Wilderness follows Caney Creek for approximately nine miles, crossing it several times. Here a thirsty hiker fills his canteen from the stream.

FLORIDA

Florida is more well known for its sun, sand and surf than for its wilderness areas, although huge Everglades National Park is famous for its unusual flora and fauna. Florida does have perhaps the best developed canoe trail system in the South, and, when completed, the 700-mile Florida Trail will lead backpackers from the Panhandle to the 'Glades on one of the country's longest continuous hiking trails.

The state's bird life is legendary, and two essential items in every outdoorsman's duffle should be a pair of binoculars and a bird identification guidebook. Winter is an excellent time to visit the state, for many northern species migrate to Florida to escape the cold weather.

In recent years, the different seasons have been more distinct in the Sunshine State, with freezing temperatures and even snow reported in Miami. Nevertheless, the months between December and April are prime times for outdoor activities since bugs and insects are gone and temperatures overall are cooler.

The State Department of Commerce News Bureau in Tallahassee is an excellent starting point for planning any outdoor activities in Florida, for they keep an updated file on nearly all recreational developments in the state.

CANOEING THE WILDERNESS WATERWAY

"Paddling among the Mangroves"

For many, the mention of Everglades National Park brings visions of waving saw grass, prairies, alligators and raised boardwalks leading across marshy canals. There is another part of the 'Glades, along Florida's Gulf Coast, where you will not find any of these things. Instead, you will be able to paddle a canoe through a maze of winding channels, pitch your tent on 2000-year-old Indian campsites and observe wildlife at paddle-length distance.

This is the Wilderness Waterway, a 100-mile canoe and boat trail marked by the National Park Service between Everglades City and Flamingo. The route leads through the mangrove jungles of the Ten Thousand Islands, across wide, shallow fish-filled bays, and along the edge of the open Gulf.

This portion of Everglades National Park is far different from the more commonly visited sections of the Tamiami Trail and Alligator Alley. There are no roads, no tourist shops, not even any drinking water. The only way in — or out — is by small boat or canoe. Instead of vast grasslands, the primary flora is mangrove. These trees grow in tangled jungles so dense Christopher Columbus, viewing them in 1494, is said to have described them as "so thick a rabbit could scarcely pass through."

There are few alligators for the water is brackish — part salt, part fresh — and the big reptiles remain further inland. There are birds, however, huge armies of shoreline waders, the endangered Everglade kite, brown pelican, bald eagle and scores of others. Crowded rookeries can also be found here.

The National Park Service maintains numerous campsites along the Wilderness Waterway, most located on old shell mounds used by Indians centuries ago. These mounds are the only high, dry spots along the waterway.

Small boats or canoes are the best craft to use when visiting the Wilderness Waterway, for some of the narrow creeks and canals are watery corridors with ceilings of low-hanging mangrove branches. There is no fast water or rapids, and no portages are required. Paddle power is slow and quiet, too, allowing travelers to truly discover the wonders of this unusual ecosystem.

The mangroves appear in three varieties—black, red and white. The black mangrove is the most unusual, seemingly unable to decide if it wants to live in the water or on land, in fresh or saltwater. It compromises, growing in tangled profusion on the shorelines, sending out cypress-like root systems into the water. And if you closely examine the underside of a black mangrove leaf, you will find excreted salt crystals.

Along the Shark River, approximately two-thirds of the way down the waterway from Everglades City, the mangroves were once among the tallest in the world, reaching heights of nearly 100 feet. More then half the forest was destroyed in 1960 by Hurricane Donna's high winds, but in time these trees will grow back.

All along the waterway there are signs of man's presence, but they are only noticeable if you look closely. Most are simply higher islands—built up by centuries of use by the Calusa Indians who inhabited this area as early as 2000 years ago. They were hunters and fishermen, living off the abundant wildlife, fish and shells. Their village sites became mounds of discarded shells. Little else remains of their civilization. The Calusas resisted the Spanish explorers for a while, and in one battle in 1521, famed navigator Ponce de Leon was mortally wounded by the Calusas; he died shortly afterward. By the end of the 18th century the Calusas had completely disappeared, and archaeologists and anthropologists still do not know what happened to them.

Some hardy white settlers have lived in this part of the Everglades, carving homesteads out of the mangroves or building small cabins on the shell mounds. Today these settlers have also gone, but old home foundations, cisterns and fence lines can still be found.

Since the settlers and the Indians lived on the highest ground around, these sites are now used as campgrounds by the National Park Service. The sites offer little more than a dry spot to pitch a tent, and possibly picnic tables and grills. Wherever the sites are located, however, campers are likely to be visited by raccoons, the most commonly seen mammal along the waterway. The animals will make their visits in daylight hours as well as under cover of darkness, so be sure to keep food inside the tent.

Bird life is always present, and canoeists will see shallow oyster reefs and mud flats teeming with an assortment of herons, egrets, ibises and spoonbills. Osprey nests are easily distinguished — massive stick and mud structures located high in the tallest trees around. A bald eagle might be seen winging overhead or an Everglade kite observed as it searches for its only food, the tiny apple snail.

Two of the more commonly seen birds are the brown pelican and the double-crested cormorant. The pelicans will be skimming low over the bays searching for fish, or perched precariously in the mangroves. The cormorants likewise may often be seen in the mangroves drying their wings, for they dive and swim underwater to catch their fish.

The Wilderness Waterway crosses 18 major bays between Everglades City and Flamingo, and one of them, Alligator Bay, is nearly salt free, although the Gulf of Mexico is but a short distance away. This brackish water zone, found all along the coast, forms one of the richest ecosystems known. Everything has its niche and its need in the overall cycle of life. Even the tremendous swarms of mosquitoes, bane of outdoorsmen everywhere, are important here. The tiny larvae are eaten by small baitfish, while the larger mosquitoes form an important part of the diet of birds and frogs.

The most enjoyable time of the year to visit this part of the Everglades is between January and April, when the mosquitos are not quite so numerous. The temperatures are still warm, the fishing can be good and the skies are only occasionally filled with thunderstorms. But the summer months bring higher temperatures and humidity, with hordes of mosquitoes.

Campers must plan on taking everything they need with them when traveling the Wilderness Waterway. It is wise to take supplies for a couple of extra days in case there is trouble in the backcountry, and it is recommended that all overnight travelers register an itinerary with National Park Service personnel.

Many of the campsites have resident raccoon populations.

HOW TO VISIT THE WILDERNESS WATERWAY

Florida's Wilderness Waterway portion of Everglades National Park can only be visited by boat or canoe. The 100-mile route marked by the National Park Service through the Ten Thousand Islands winds from Everglades City on the Gulf of Mexico to the small town of Flamingo on Florida Bay. Although marked with mileage posts, the region is a maze of look-alike bays, winding rivers, canals and mangrove-covered islands. Travelers leaving the main waterway without a navigation chart can easily end up lost. Boaters must also be aware of the hazards of rapidly changing depths caused by shell bars and fluctuating tides.

This is a waterway for small boats, and canoeists are especially welcome. Boats longer than 18 feet, and those craft with high cabins or windshields, will encounter problems in the narrow channels and with overhanging mangrove branches. The complete trip of 100 miles takes a full day by outboard, or about seven days by canoe.

BOATING AND CANOEING: The ideal way to visit the Wilderness Waterway is by canoe, whether for just a portion of the 100-mile route, or to make the entire Everglades City-Flamingo run. There are no white-water rapids; the only paddling problem is wind in the more open bays. Canoeists will have no trouble crossing the shallow reefs that stop larger motor boats, nor will they encounter any problems in negotiating the tight twisty turns of some creeks and channels.

Canoeists will have to pack all equipment with them, including drinking water, for none is available in the backcountry. It is wise to pack one life preserver per person and an extra paddle for each canoe. Trips should be scheduled with at least two canoes.

Although many paddle the entire waterway without guides, first-time visitors may wish to take guided package trips. One of the most well-known outfitters in the region is Tex Stout, owner of Canoe Outpost, Inc., Rt. 2, Box 330-J, Sarasota, FL 33582. Tex schedules three to four trips a year, each lasting four days. Paddlers must furnish their own food, clothing and personal items; he provides canoes, tents, cooking stoves, drinking water and eating utensils. The cost is approximately

$44.00 per person per day.

The Canoe Outpost trips begin and end at Everglades City, and paddlers may key their trips to fishing, sightseeing or wildlife photography. Each of these regularly scheduled trips is in March and April before the mosquitoes and heat become too oppressive, but Tex will schedule groups of ten people during January and February on the days of their choice, with prices the same.

Short canoe trips are also offered on occasion by the National Park Service. Information is available from the Superintendent, Everglades National Park, P.O. Box 279, Homestead, FL 33030.

Spare gasoline and an assortment of tools for emergency repairs are recommended items for motorboats. Special attention must be given to tides and shallow reefs, for running aground may mean a wait of 12 hours before the next high water. Boaters also need to take insect repellent, sunburn lotion and rain gear. Temperatures will be in the 80s and 90s, with afternoon storms a possibility. Mosquitoes are bad on the mangrove islands after dark.

CAMPING: There are 17 backcountry campsites along the 100-mile waterway, all available free of charge and on a first-come, first-served basis. The sites consist primarily of cleared shell islands where tents may be pitched, and picnic tables and grills are usually provided. Open campfires may be built, but the use of portable stoves is strongly recommended.

The campsites are marked by signs and are easily located on the region's major bays and rivers. While most are inland, several are situated on the open Gulf. The following U.S. Coast and Geodetic Charts are helpful when navigating the Wilderness Waterway and show the campsite locations: Charts No. 1254 or 642-SC, 1253 or 642-SC, 598-SC and 599-SC. These charts are available in Everglades City and in Flamingo.

Between December 1 and April 30 — the best time for Everglades canoeing — camping is limited to 14 days. During the other remaining months, camping is limited to 30 days.

FISHING AND HUNTING: No hunting is permitted within Everglades National Park.

Fishing, at certain times of the year, can be excellent. The mangrove waterways are home for snook, speckled trout, redfish and tarpon. No fishing licenses are required. Anglers plan-

Much of the waterway winds along narrow mangrove-lined creeks and channels. Fishing is good but mosquitoes bad during the summer months. The best time for a Wilderness Waterway trip is in the winter.

ning to fish this area need to carry saltwater spinning tackle or fairly heavy freshwater outfits. Artificial lures should include a variety of noisy top-water plugs for snook, gold and silver spoons for redfish, small swimming/diving plugs and hair jigs for trout. Tarpon may hit plugs and jigs. Monofilament line testing 14 pounds or stronger is recommended, with the last three feet of line doubled to act as a leader. Line must be checked often for fraying as it is pulled over the shells and mangrove roots.

Snook will hide in the shallow water of the mangrove banks, and redfish may be seen "tailing" over some of the mud flats. Trout can be caught in some of the deeper channels, and tarpon might surface in the cuts and passes during a changing tide. Each of these species can be caught during the spring months, but snook are caught more regularly later in summer.

WILDLIFE OBSERVATION: The Everglades is well known for its abundant bird life, and visitors in the Ten Thousand Islands and Wilderness Waterway can expect to see nesting ospreys, flamingos, egrets, ibises, herons and possibly an Everglade kite. About 80 bird species nest in the Everglades, and more than 300 species have been observed and identified here.

Paddlers will see raccoons around the campsites; care should be taken to protect food and camping equipment. Deer are here but seldom seen, as are bobcat and panther.

Do not look for alligators in this part of the 'Glades, for they are found more frequently in the eastern portions of the park, in the saw grass prairies. Though rarely seen there are about two dozen species of snakes in the Everglades, only four of which are poisonous.

ADDITIONAL INFORMATION: Additional information is available from the Superintendent, Everglades National Park, P.O. Box 279, Homestead, FL 33030.

An excellent guidebook to the region is "A Guide to the Wilderness Waterway of the Everglades National Park," by William G. Truesdell. It is available in Flamingo and in Everglades City at the National Park offices.

A brown pelican, one of America's endangered species, sits atop a mangrove watching as canoeists pass. These huge birds are frequently seen along the waterway.

GEORGIA

Hikers, campers and river runners have much to choose from in Georgia. The southern tip of the Appalachians extends into the state, dropping gradually into rolling hills and finally into coastal plain. Much of the northern half of Georgia is embraced within the Chattahoochee National Forest, which contains the federally protected Cohutta Wilderness.

Unfortunately, the Cohutta receives heavy usage, especially from backpackers and campers from Atlanta and Chattanooga. The wilderness trail system there does help spread people out, but a busy summer weekend will see trailheads crowded with automobiles and scenic sites full of tents; it is a great place for meeting new friends. Weekday usage is much less.

Atlanta is the metropolitan hub of the South and, as befitting the growing popularity of wilderness sports, has many different shops specializing in camping, hiking and paddling equipment. Many provide guided weekend trips into the Chattahoochee, and special clinics for newcomers are frequently offered.

Summer weather often includes hot humid days with afternoon and evening showers. Winter in the mountains will be cold. Spring rains cause river trail crossings to be difficult, while fall turns the forests into a rainbow of colors.

THE CHATTOOGA RIVER

"Paddling the River of Deliverance*"*

Whiteside Mountain, near the small mountain village of Cashiers, North Carolina, is popular among tourists because it overlooks two small but scenic lakes, Silver Slip and Cashiers. The overflow from these lakes produces two equally spectacular waterfalls, which in turn produce one of the most awesome rivers in the Southeast, the Chattooga.

Whenever the roll call of rivers is read, the Chattooga is listed beside such famous waters as the Colorado, Green and Salmon. Like these Western rivers, the Chattooga is a whitewater river for experienced canoeists, kayakers and rafters. Rapids here rate to a rugged Class 5, and for much of its 49-mile length the river is cradled in a deep wilderness gorge with extremely limited access. Once on the water, a paddler is committed to the river.

This wilderness—heavily forested mountain slopes, steep rocky canyons, churning rapids, abundant wildlife and a virtual lack of human habitation—was one of the first rivers ever designated "Wild and Scenic" by Congress. Even though the well-known movie *Deliverance* was filmed here, the Chattooga remains wild, free and unforgiving.

From its origin in Cashiers, the Chattooga flows southward for about 10 miles, gaining strength from several small feeder creeks and springs. Leaving North Carolina, the river then becomes the state boundary between Georgia and South Carolina for the next 40 miles until it is finally absorbed by Lake Tugaloo near the town of Tallulah Falls, Georgia.

While most paddlers are rightfully concerned about safely negotiating the river's many rapids, they are rewarded for their efforts if they try. The Chattooga flows through a lush forest wonderland, rich in flora and fauna. An annual rainfall of 100 inches provides ideal conditions for rhododendron, mountain laurel, dogwood, pine, hemlock, oak and ash, as well as colorful wildflowers and exotic ferns. Botanists say the Chattooga watershed contains more varieties of trees than all of Europe. Quiet paddlers may see deer, bear, wild turkey, fox and beaver near the river's edge. The harmonious "bob-white" call of the quail and the haunting "coo" of the mourning dove are also frequently heard along the river's quiet stretches.

For years, the Chattooga churned relatively unnoticed through this wilderness setting, visited only occasionally by local white-water paddlers, intrepid backpackers and trout fishermen. It was not until Hollywood filmed its popular movie *Deliverance* here that the Chattooga really became known to the rest of the world. That film, adapted from the James Dickey novel and starring well-known actors Jon Voight and Burt Reynolds, not only helped popularize wild river canoeing, but also brought a flood of paddlers to the Chattooga.

Many of those paddlers were inexperienced, too, and found the boiling rapids far too much for them. Nearly two dozen people are reported to have drowned in the river, and many, many more have left broken canoes and punctured rafts on the rocks and falls. Today the U.S. Forest Service, who helps administer and control traffic on the Chattooga, strictly enforces various safety regulations that have greatly reduced river accidents.

Paddlers have divided the Chattooga into four separate sections for canoeing and rafting. These are based on river access (or escape!) points, and range in distance from 6 to 16 miles.

Section One begins at Cashiers and continues to Russell Bridge at Ga. Highway 28. This portion of the Chattooga is not recommended for canoeing or rafting, due to strenuous portaging through heavy forest underbrush. The river is narrow and filled with rocks as it cascades down through the North Carolina highlands. The only canoeing on Section One is a 2.5-mile stretch between Nicholson Ford and Ga. 28 where the water is calm.

Section Two is extremely popular with novice canoeists and is the only portion of the Chattooga where inner tubes are allowed. Beginning at Ga. 28 bridge and continuing seven miles to Earl's Ford on Whetstone Road, this is primarily a quiet water section that contains only two major rapids, Turn

Hole and Big Shoals.

Turn Hole is a sweeping right-hander where the river pulls canoeists to the outside bank and seldom presents any major problems. Big Shoals is classified as a Class 3 rapid and requires a bit more maneuvering through rocks for a short distance.

Section Three begins at Earl's Ford, the takeout point for Section Two, and continues downstream 13 miles to the U.S. Highway 76 bridge. The rapids begin almost immediately and rate up to Class 5 before the takeout point is reached. Because much of this portion of the river flows through a steep-walled gorge, paddlers along Section Three are committed to completing the run once they start. Several scenes from *Deliverance* were filmed here, and in a couple of spots the remains of old canoes can still be seen.

Many paddlers run into trouble here at a set of rapids known as The Narrows, where the river cuts through a 150-yard-long rocky cliffside and actually flows under some of the overhanging rocks. High waves and wicked crosscurrents combine to swamp many a canoe on this run. Other well-known rapids following include Eye of the Needle, Roller Coaster and

Chattooga River canoeists study a rapid from the bank before attempting to run it. Life jackets should be worn at all times on the Chattooga, and many canoeists wear safety helmets.

Painted Rock, all of which have seen their share of swamped canoes. Just above the U.S. 76 bridge is the most rugged rapid of this section, Bull Sluice, rated Class 5. Many believe the best way to run this rapid is on foot, portaging over the rocks, which in itself is a challenge.

Bull Sluice has claimed the lives of several paddlers who underestimated its ferocity; this rapid should always be studied from the shore before running. The approach is rated Class 3, which gets a lot of people into trouble. A five-foot drop puts canoes only halfway through the storm. A second drop follows the first, but not before paddlers must get free of a massive boat-breaking hydraulic wave. If that is not enough, there is a huge unforgiving rock hidden about halfway through the sluice.

Section Four is for experienced paddlers only, and is generally rated as the premier white-water run in the Southeast. Although this portion of the river is only 7.5-miles long, it churns all the way and is not recommended for open canoes. This section begins at the U.S. 76 bridge crossing and continues to Lake Tugaloo. Expect to take a full day for this portion.

The Chattooga is also popular with paddlers in decked canoes and kayaks. Here two river runners challenge Section Three.

The first rapid begins "right around the bend" after putting in at the bridge. Named Surfing Rapid, it is a Class 3, some of the calmest white water of Section Four. Many scenes from *Deliverance* were filmed along this portion of the river, including several at the very next rapid, Screaming Left Turn, a long stretch of foaming waves and rocks.

One of the most dangerous rapids on the river is Woodall Shoals, more than 200 feet of falls, hydraulic waves and boulders. This Class 5 rapid has caused several deaths and, like Bull Sluice on Section Three, is best run by going over the rocks with the canoe on your shoulders.

And, as Section Three ends with Bull Sluice, Section Four ends with an awesome stretch of white water, too — 0.3 mile of five consecutive rapids ranging in difficulty from Class 3 to Class 5. The first is known appropriately as Entrance Rapid (Class 3 and 4), consisting of two three-foot drops and a long garden of rocks. Next in line are Corkscrew (Class 5), Crack-in-the-Rock (Class 4 and 5), Jawbone (Class 4 and 5), Sock-'Em-Dog (Class 4 and 5) and Shoulder Bone (Class 3). From this last rapid, it is just a short paddle to Lake Tugaloo, although the takeout point is approximately two miles down the lake on the South Carolina shore.

Experts regularly raft and canoe the Chattooga without serious mishaps. Beginners and moderately skilled paddlers should not attempt this river unless accompanied by experienced personnel or licensed guides. The U.S. Forest Service has licensed only three outfitters to lead commercial canoe and raft trips down the Chattooga, and each of these licenses are reviewed annually. Safety regulations require the wearing of life preservers at all times, wearing safety helmets on Section Four and assuring that all rafts have at least two separate air compartments.

HOW TO VISIT THE CHATTOOGA RIVER

Unless you plan to paddle the river itself, the best places to see the Chattooga are from the bridge crossings on Ga. 28 between Walhalla, South Carolina and Highlands, North Carolina; and on U.S. 76 between Westminster, South Carolina, and Clayton, Georgia. The U.S. 76 crossing marks the end of Section Three and the beginning of Section Four. A short walk upstream leads to Bull Sluice rapid, and a short hike downstream reaches Surfing Rapid.

There are other landings or fords of the river, reached by following U.S. Forest Service roads. Maps showing these roads are available from the Supervisor, Sumter National Forest, 1801 Assembly Street, Columbia, SC 29201.

CANOEING AND RAFTING: These, of course, are the best ways to see the river, and guided raft trips are offered on both Sections Three and Four by licensed outfitters during the spring and summer months. The outfitters are: Nantahala Outdoor Center, Star Route, Box 68, Bryson City, NC 28713; Southeastern Expeditions, 2220 Parklake Drive N.E., Suite 330, Atlanta, GA 30345; and Wildwater Ltd., Long Creek, SC 29658 (winter address: 400 West Road, Portsmouth, VA 23707).

On guided raft trips all paddles, safety helmets and life preservers are furnished and lunch is included. A guide rides on board each raft, but everyone joins in the paddling. It is a wet ride and not recommended for people who cannot swim or who are afraid of rough water.

Guided canoe trips are offered by the same outfitters, but paddlers must have previous white-water canoeing experience. Again, all necessary safety equipment, paddles and canoes are furnished.

FISHING AND HUNTING: The Chattooga provides challenging trout fishing, simply by virtue of its inaccessibility. Most anglers concentrate on Sections One and Two of the river, as well as some of its tributary creeks.

Hunting is permitted during season for deer, quail, squirrel and other game in both Chattahoochee (Georgia) and Sumter (South Carolina) national forests through which the Chattooga flows. No loaded firearms are permitted within 0.5 mile of a national forest campground. Hunting and fishing regulations are available from the Georgia Department of Natural Resources, 270 Washington Street SW, Atlanta, GA 30334; and from the South Carolina Wildlife and Marine Resources Department, Box 167, Columbia, SC 29202.

WILDLIFE OBSERVATION: The rugged terrain surrounding the Chattooga River for nearly all its length provides ideal habitat for a wide variety of animal life, including whitetail deer, black bear, wild turkey, wild boar, squirrel, fox, raccoon

Bull Sluice marks the end of Section Three on the Chattooga, and most believe the best way to run this rapid is over the rocks with the canoe on your shoulders. Here a lone paddler tries the water route. The white blocks in the canoe are for extra flotation.

and beaver. River paddlers may see some of these species at water's edge during early morning or late evening hours. Backpackers may see deer or bear along some of the trails lacing through the region.

HIKING AND BACKPACKING: Several trails lead through the national forests to the river and along its banks. One popular trail leads 4.5 miles from the Walhalla Fish Hatchery to Ellicott's Rock, marking the boundary of North Carolina, South Carolina and Georgia.

CAMPING: Several campgrounds are open in the vicinity of the Chattooga. These include two in the Sumter National Forest, Burrell's Ford and Cherry Hill, both off S.C. Highway 107. Burrell's Ford, located on the river, is accessible only on foot and is for hikers and fishermen only. It offers 9 tent sites. Cherry Hill provides 25 sites for both tents and RV users, and includes showers. Fees for either area are $2.00 to $3.00 per night. Oconee State Park is further from the river, but is also located on S.C. 107 and provides 140 sites for tents and RVs.

ADDITIONAL INFORMATION: Additional information on the Chattooga is available from the U.S Forest Service, Star Route, Walhalla, SC 29691. River maps are available for $.50 from this source.

THE COHUTTA WILDERNESS
"Georgia's Wild and Rugged Mountains"

The 667,000-acre Chattahoochee National Forest, sprawling across the north Georgia mountains to the South Carolina state line, ranks as one of the South's premier outdoor recreation areas, and a part of this forest, the 34,000-acre Cohutta Wilderness, is one of the largest tracts set aside for wilderness preservation. This is a rugged region, with elevations ranging from less than 1000 feet to over 4000 feet, steep bluffs, heavily timbered ridges and wild, cascading rivers. The Jacks and Conasauga rivers have their headwaters here, and both support fine populations of native wild trout. Backpacking trails crisscross each of these rivers, while others climb over mountains, follow sharp summit ridges or meander through steep-walled valleys.

Like virtually all southern forests, the Cohutta region has been logged. During a 20-year span earlier in this century, more than half of what is now the wilderness was cut. The timber companies were after chestnut primarily, and occasionally a mossy stump can be found as evidence of past lumbering operations. Those trees the loggers missed were killed by the chestnut blight that swept across the Southeast in the 1930s.

Although the chestnut are gone, the Cohutta still supports a wide variety of forest flora. Because of the sharp elevation change in such a short distance, hikers can literally walk from the sandy-soiled warm-weather pine plantations to mountain ridge hardwood stands. In between, the forest growth may be a mixture of yellow poplar and hemlock, with a thick understory of rhododendron. Botanists have identified more than 40 species of rare plants in the wilderness — evidence that this portion of the Appalachians has greater plant and timber diversity than almost any other region of North America.

Backpackers will find a degree of diversity in the wildlife, too. Whitetail deer, once nearly wiped out in Georgia, are common in the Cohutta Wilderness today. Bear prowl the bluffs and high ridges but are seldom seen. In the spring a careful listener at dawn will probably hear the short rolling gobble of a tom turkey and in the fall may encounter small flocks of the big black birds. Riverside campsites might be visited by raccoons, and chipmunks will scamper along the forest floor during the summer in their search for nuts and berries.

Two of the most noticeable features of the Cohutta are its major rivers, the Conasauga and Jacks. Both are boulder-strewn waterways that change abruptly from quiet pools to surging falls. These rivers have wide-reaching tributary systems, and even during traditional summer low-water conditions, fording them can be a treacherous undertaking. After heavy rains in early spring crossing can be extremely dangerous.

Backpacking trails follow both the Jacks and Conasauga rivers, and numerous crossings are required along each route. Other trails follow smaller streams and also include wet crossings. There are over 70 miles of old logging roads through the wilderness, but not all trails follow them.

Because of its close proximity to several million people, the Cohutta Wilderness receives heavy weekend use during the spring and summer months. An extended backcountry trip during the week, however, will probably result in solitude and complete enjoyment of this rugged region.

HOW TO VISIT THE COHUTTA WILDERNESS

The Cohutta Wilderness is tucked into the northern part of Georgia, straddling Murray and Fannin counties. This part of the Chattahoochee National Forest is within easy driving distance of Chattanooga and Atlanta, and indeed, the majority of the Cohutta's visitors probably come from these two cities.

The wilderness is reached by following Interstate 75 south from Chattanooga to Ringgold, Georgia, and exiting there on

Even in summer backpackers find the many crossings of the Conasauga River wet. The Conasauga Trail crosses the river several dozen times in its 14-mile span of the wilderness.

to Ga. Highway 2, which leads to the wilderness just outside the small town of Cisco. Once in this part of the national forest the road is no longer paved and is recommended for trucks and four-wheel drive vehicles only, especially after heavy rains. Hikers and campers may drive their automobiles to the various trailheads, however, with little difficulty in dry weather.

HIKING AND BACKPACKING: The Cohutta Wilderness is laced with trails and several of them intersect so loop trip variations are possible. Some of these trails follow old logging roads and are not strenuous; others wind up and down mountain ridges and are for experienced backpackers only; still others follow streams and have frequent wet crossings. The area is bordered by Forest Service roads where trailheads are located.

One well-known trail, the Jacks River Trail, follows the Jacks River for approximately 14 miles, crossing the river more than 40 times. Even during times of low water, backpackers can expect to get their knees wet on this trail. Another well-used trail, the Beech Bottom Trail, does not have any challenging water crossings, but does lead 4 miles down to Jacks River Falls, one of the more spectacular waterfalls in the wilderness. This trail is a former logging road most of the way and is easy hiking.

A more rugged hike is possible on the Tearbritches Trail, a three-miler leading up over the summit of Bald Mountain. Along its length this path climbs from 2000 feet to over 4000 feet in elevation.

Other trails in the Cohutta Wilderness include the Conasauga, Hickory Ridge, Horseshoe Bend, Penitentiary Branch, Rough Ridge and East Cowpen trails. Trail signs may be infrequent, so maps should be used. There are no shelters on any of these trails, but suitable tent sites are plentiful. Water can be dipped from the streams but should be purified.

CAMPING: Camping is permitted anywhere within the wilderness, and fires are permitted. No permits are required. Backpackers should plan on using portable stoves whenever possible to minimize harmful effects on the environment. Along most of the trails evidence of past camps is clearly visible.

Basic camping gear here should include rainwear for use during sudden mountain showers and possibly a snakebite kit.

The Cohutta Wilderness contains many species of wildlife, including black bear, deer and wild turkey.

HUNTING AND FISHING: Hunting is permitted in season for deer, turkey, wild boar, ruffed grouse and various species of small game. At times special deer hunts are conducted in the region for trophy bucks only. These are permit-only hunts, lasting one or two days.

Fishing is good in the Cohutta for rainbow, brown and brook trout, and for Coosa bass, a cousin of the largemouth bass. Special trout fishing regulations may be in effect on some of the Cohutta waters, but all anglers will need a Georgia fishing license as well as a trout stamp.

For additional information, contact the Georgia Department of Natural Resources, 270 Washington St. SW, Atlanta, GA 30334.

WILDLIFE OBSERVATION: Observant campers may see whitetail deer along the forested ridges, and possibly a turkey or even a bear in the remote areas of the wilderness. Smaller animals including chipmunks and squirrels are common. More than 300 species of birds have been identified in the Chattahoochee National Forest, most of them migrants passing through at various seasons of the year. Hawks are common throughout the year, as are various other woodland species.

ADDITIONAL INFORMATION: Additional information on the Cohutta Wilderness is available from the Supervisor, Chattahoochee National Forest, 601 Broad St. NE, Gainesville, GA 30501; or from the Cohutta District Ranger, U.S. Forest Service, Chatsworth, GA 30705.

OKEFENOKEE SWAMP
"Land of the Trembling Earth"

Half a million years ago, time stopped in a small corner of southeast Georgia. It is still trying to catch up.

That small corner of the state is the Okefenokee Swamp, a 435,000-acre wilderness of water, craggy cypress and alligators. Even though the Okefenokee is surrounded on all sides by man's modern technology, visiting the swamp is like stepping back thousands of years into time.

Actually, the Okefenokee is not a true swamp. Its land stands higher in elevation than that surrounding it in nearby towns of Fargo and Waycross. And while much of the Okefenokee consists of water, it is not still, stagnant water as in most swamps. A current moves constantly; in fact, the water tests pure enough to drink. Two major southern rivers, the Suwannee and the St. Marys, begin in the Okefenokee.

There is very little mud here, either, another contradiction of the popular notion of a swamp. Beneath the water there is hard white sand, for the Okefenokee actually had its beginning as ocean floor. During the Pleistocene era, between 500,000 and 1,250,000 years ago, the Atlantic Ocean covered this part of Georgia. Through continuous wave and current fluctuation, a 100-mile long sand bar known as Trail Ridge was formed. When the ocean later receded to give the Eastern Seaboard its present configuration, some ocean water was trapped behind this long sand bar. This trapped water soon became a huge freshwater lake as rains washed away the salt, and eventually aquatic plants took root. The centuries passed and these plants grew, died and decayed, sinking to the lake floor where they gradually became peat. These peat deposits continued to accumulate in the shallow water, forming the growing base for other aquatic vegetation. Sedges, shrubs, and finally cypress and gum trees began to grow in them.

Thus the Okefenokee Swamp was born.

Because the peat never firmly anchored itself to the lake floor but floated in the water instead, it did not become solid. Even today you can find places where the ground trembles to the step and entire trees shake with a heavy footfall. This unusual characteristic has given the Okefenokee its famous nickname, "Land of the Trembling Earth."

Some of the peat islands did become anchored as tree roots grew down into the sand. There are less than 75 of these "permanent" islands in the Okefenokee, the largest measuring about nine miles long and one mile wide.

In addition to these islands, the Okefenokee today consists of three more distinct types of terrain: the open marshy prairies, the soggy hammocks and the cypress belts. The prairies sometimes stretch for miles, appearing as a rich, colorful carpet of lilies, canes and ferns. These plants are growing in wild profusion in the water and cannot support the weight of a person.

The hammocks are actually a formation stage of the permanent islands. Most are covered with a wide variety of berries, bushes and primary forest trees such as pine. In years to come, these hammocks will give way to the cypress belts. The cypress here grow at the rate of about a foot a year, but barring disease or fire, will live for centuries.

In the early part of this century, attempts were made to harvest the Okefenokee's cypress, and over a 20-year period approximately nine million board feet of timber were taken from the swamp. A lumberman names Charles Hebard, constructing a small town on Billy's Island in the swamp, pushed a railroad some 35 miles through the Okefenokee, laying train rails atop 20-foot pilings driven through the peat into the underlying sand.

Hebard paid his men $2.50 a day with tokens that could be redeemed for merchandise in his town. The village was completely self-contained, with a school, commissary, hotel and even a movie theater. The town doctor drove a Model T Ford to visit his patients, putting train wheels on the vehicle so he could drive it on the railroad tracks.

The start of the Great Depression in 1929 brought a halt to Okefenokee logging operations, and in 1936 the federal government purchased the Okefenokee for $1.50 per acre. The following year 293,000 acres were designated as a National Wildlife Refuge to protect the region's abundant wildlife.

Alligators are the most noticeable of the Okefenokee's residents, simply because they are so large. But over 40 species of mammals live here, including black bear, deer, fox, bobcat and raccoon. Some 210 species of birds have been recorded in the Okefenokee, many of which nest in the swamp. There are 14 kinds of turtles, lizards ranging in size from three inches to three feet in length and frogs only as large as a dime. There are over 30 species of fish here, too, with largemouth bass, bluegill and catfish the most popular among anglers.

In years past, poaching activities nearly wiped out the Okefenokee's alligator population. Former U.S. Fish and Wildlife Service game ranger Barney Cone, who spent 28 years in the Okefenokee, often had to arrest his friends and neighbors who attempted to shoot the alligators and then sell the hides for as much as $6.50 per foot. During one stakeout, Cone and his partner watched a poacher's boat for 30 straight nights, waiting to apprehend the owner who never came. Finally, in frustration, Cone and his fellow agent burned the

One of the frequently seen residents of the Okefenokee is the alligator, which often swims with just its head above water. Poachers nearly wiped out the swamp's 'gator population just a few years ago, but with federal protection the alligator is again increasing in numbers.

Water lilies grow in wild profusion in the Okefenokee's waterways, and in spring form a green carpet filled with white flowers.

boat on the 31st night. He had his own memorable experiences, too, with the alligators he fought so hard to protect. Once he accidentally stepped on a gator while wading through thigh-deep water. Cone lost the seat of his pants to the gator's jaws before he could get free.

Long before the poachers and lumbermen came to the Okefenokee, however, the swamp had been inhabited by man. The first was a group of mound builders who lived far in the interior prior to the 16th century. Another tribe, the Yuchis or "Children of the Sun," lived in the Okefenokee from about 1600 to 1682. They were followed by the Seminoles, who remained until 1838 when General Charles Floyd drove them out.

Today, little evidence of any of these tribes remains. The lumber town on Billy's Island burned, leaving the Okefenokee free to return completely to nature, which, with the help of the U.S. Fish and Wildlife Service protection, the swamp has done.

HOW TO VISIT THE OKEFENOKEE

The three entrances into the Okefenokee are Stephen C. Foster State Park near Fargo, Suwannee Canal Recreation Area near Folkston and Okefenokee Swamp Park near Waycross. Stephen Foster State Park is located 17 miles northeast of Fargo off Ga. Highway 177. Okefenokee Swamp Park is 8 miles south of Waycross off U.S. Highways 1 and 23. Admission is charged. Suwannee Canal Recreation Area is 8 miles southwest of Folkston on Ga. 23.

CANOEING: There are six designated wilderness canoe trails lacing through the Okefenokee, offering numerous trip variations. Each canoe trail is limited to one party daily, and each party is limited to a maximum of ten canoes and/or 20 persons. Permits are required and may be obtained from the refuge manager. Reservations should be made several weeks in advance. Guides are not needed.

Camping is permitted only at designated overnight stops, consisting of 20' X 28' raised wooden platforms. Open fires are permitted only at certain locations, and portable toilets with disposable bags are required.

Canoes may be rented from the Concessioner, Suwannee Canal Recreation Area, Folkston, GA 31537. Canoes for daily use only may be rented at Stephen C. Foster State Park and Suwannee Canal Recreation Area; each canoe is equipped with life preservers and paddles.

FISHING AND HUNTING: No hunting is permitted. Fishing is excellent for largemouth bass, black crappie and numerous species of sunfish, including bluegill and redbreast. Live minnows are not permitted as bait in the Okefenokee.

Fishing guides may be hired by reservation only at Okefenokee Swamp Park.

WILDLIFE OBSERVATION: Sightseeing trips by boat are conducted daily by personnel at Stephen Foster State Park, Okefenokee Swamp Park and Suwannee Canal Recreation Area. The admission fee at Okefenokee Swamp Park includes a two-mile boat ride, but longer trips with guides may be arranged. Guided sightseeing trips lasting up to a full day can be arranged through the concessioner at Suwannee Canal Recreation Area.

Fine opportunities to observe wildlife are available along raised swamp boardwalks at Okefenokee Swamp Park and Suwannee Canal Recreation Area. At Stephen Foster State Park, many varieties of bird and animal life are frequently seen in the campground. The Suwannee Canal Recreation Area also features a special wildlife drive for automobiles.

On any of these trips expect to see alligators and several species of birds, such as the white ibis, American egret and great blue heron. During the winter the Okefenokee is alive with waterfowl, while the summer months bring some warblers, wrens and many of the wading varieties. Reptiles and amphibians including lizards, turtles, salamanders and frogs are more commonly seen than mammals. Whitetail deer are common near the Stephen C. Foster State Park campground.

Canoeists wind among the cypress as they explore the Okefenokee's narrow waterways. Canoe trails are well marked, and overnight trips are extremely popular.

WILD PLACES OF THE SOUTH

CAMPING: Stephen C. Foster State Park offers the only over-night facilities in the Okefenokee. The large campground features sites for tents, trailers or RVs and has several cottages for rent. At the other two Okefenokee entrances, hours of operation are during daylight only. There are no overnight backpacking trails in these areas.

ADDITIONAL INFORMATION: For additional information, contact one of these sources: Stephen C. Foster State Park, Fargo, GA 31631; Suwannee Canal Recreation Area, Folkston, GA 31537; Okefenokee Swamp Park, Waycross, GA 31501; Okefenokee National Wildlife Refuge, P.O. Box 117, Waycross, GA 31501.

CUMBERLAND ISLAND
"The Enchanted Forest"

It is often said that America's earliest inhabitants, the various Indian tribes living here long before Columbus stepped ashore in 1492, knew a good place to live when they saw it. That reasoning is certainly true at Cumberland Island, Georgia, as any modern-day visitor will quickly discover. Indians inhabited this barrier island for over 3000 years, beginning about 2000 B.C. and continuing through the 16th century, after the arrival of Spanish explorers. They lived off the abundant fish and wildlife of the region, and today the remains of their shell mounds, or middens, are clearly visible.

The Timucuan Indians and the Spanish were not the only people who liked Cumberland Island. The English pioneers did too, and they defeated the Spanish for control in 1742. After the Revolution, Americans took over, and now nearly all of Cumberland is owned and managed by the National Park Service as a national seashore.

Cumberland is not a large island, measuring about 16 miles long and 3 miles wide. It is, however, the largest of the "Golden Isles" of Georgia's coast, and the southernmost. To many, Cumberland is also the most enchanting of the island chain.

From the water, Cumberland first appears as a dark forest of moss-draped oaks, trees that do not grow very tall but spread low and wide over the ground instead. These are live oaks, whose limbs have been shaped by years of wind-blown salt spray. Walking beneath their tangled canopy is like entering a vast room, for it is cool and windless even at midday. A light rain shower will not penetrate the thick foliage.

The oak forest is but one of several distinct ecosystems on

Cumberland. In places the forest gives way to saltwater marsh, the rich mixing ground of cordgrass and salt where dozens of life forms live and thrive. Along the Atlantic shore, the oaks gradually surrender to the dunes—massive, slowly moving mountains of sand that in places have actually buried portions of the forest. The dunes, in turn, change to the hard sand beach of the ocean.

Of the coastal barrier islands, Cumberland has the greatest faunal and plant life diversity. Whitetail deer, squirrel, raccoon, alligators and over 300 species of birds have been identified here. This is the home of vast colonies of fiddler crabs, those inch-long speedsters that vary in color according to the sunlight; and of horseshoe crab, a creature that has changed little in 200 million years and which is actually more closely related to spiders than crabs. Huge, loggerhead turtles lumber ashore on Cumberland during the summer nights to tearfully deposit their eggs, and wild turkey peck and prowl through the palmettos. Parula warblers and painted buntings add a dash of color to the mossy limbs, while pelicans and terns keep the beaches alive with movement. Feral horses roam the marshes and beaches adding a touch of western flavor to the island.

Barrier islands are generally thought of as fragile and easily destroyed, but Cumberland has withstood human visitation well; and what people have torn down, nature has quickly rebuilt. It is difficult to believe Cumberland's mighty oaks were largely cut down just over a century ago, or that a large plantation aristocracy based on cotton once thrived here. The only signs of their presence today are the ruins of former mansions and several quiet homes still inhabited by family ancestors.

The Spanish are believed to have constructed a fort and mission on Cumberland in the late 1500s to convert the Timucuans to Catholicism. No remains of these buildings can be seen today. One hundred and fifty years later, in 1736, General James Oglethorpe, founder of Georgia's first English colony, built two forts on Cumberland, defeating the Spanish for island control. Oglethorpe also constructed a private hunting lodge named Dungeness on the southern portion of the island.

Cumberland remained essentially uninhabited, however, until after the Revolutionary War, when General Nathaneal Greene, the youngest American general in the conflict, purchased much of the island. He established logging operations on Cumberland, selling the oak as timber for the new American navy's sailing ships. Greene began building his home on Cumberland, also naming the residence Dungeness and constructing it in the same area as Oglethorpe's lodge. However, he died in 1786 without ever seeing his mansion completed. His widow, Catherine, and her second husband, Phineas Miller, finally completed the home about ten years later.

Until her death in 1814, Catherine Greene Miller controlled the life style of Cumberland Island. Her daughter, Louisa Greene Shaw, continued the agricultural work on the island, expanding the crops to include figs, olives, oranges and limes.

All that stands today of the Dungeness mansion complex built by Catherine Miller is a small tabby house, believed to have been built around 1800. The main building was destroyed by fire in 1866, after which the plantation was abandoned.

In 1881 Thomas Carnegie, brother of Andrew Carnegie, and his wife Lucy visited Cumberland and purchased much of the island. They began constructing still another Dungeness mansion on the former site of the Shaw home, but like the men before him, Thomas died before seeing it completed. Lucy Carnegie finished the building and eventually purchased about 90 percent of the island. She built four additional mansions on Cumberland for her children, developed a golf course and constructed a large recreational building complete with swimming pool, guest rooms and riding stables.

Portions of all these buildings can be seen by visitors today. The Dungeness mansion fell into disuse in the 1920s and then burned in 1959, but the brick walls and chimneys are still in place. Another mansion, named Plum Orchard, is open to visitors on National Park Service (NPS) tours, and a third mansion, Greyfield, is now a private inn operated by Carnegie descendant Lucy Ferguson.

Much of the island has been purchased by the National Park Service and established as the Cumberland Island National Seashore. Travel to and from the island is via a park service ferry, and all transportation on the island itself is by foot. It is possible to visit the Dungeness ruins on a short half-day excursion to the island, but backcountry campers and hikers have the best opportunity for exploring the island.

There are no paved roads, only one-lane dirt trails and footpaths, for visitors are not allowed to bring automobiles to the island.

A backpacker stands at the edge of the Atlantic Ocean on Cumberland's eastern shore. Hikers can walk among the dunes or follow shaded trails through the interior.

HOW TO VISIT CUMBERLAND ISLAND

Cumberland Island National Seashore can only be reached by boat or ferry. No docking facilities for private boats are available, so visitors must use either the national Park Service ferry or hire a private boat from the town of St. Marys.

To reach the park office and ferry landing in St. Marys, simply follow Ga. Highway 40 through the town until it dead ends at the water. Both the ferry and the office are there. The town of St. Marys is located in the southeastern corner of Georgia, approximately six miles east of the Interstate 95 intersection with Ga. 40. Motel accommodations, campgrounds and restaurants are available in the town.

The NPS ferry departs St. Marys at 9:15 a.m. and 1:45 p.m., arriving at the island at 10:00 a.m. and 2:30 p.m. Departures from Cumberland are at 12:15 p.m. and 4:45 p.m., arriving back in St. Marys at 1:00 p.m. and 5:30 p.m. This schedule is followed daily during the summer months of June, July and August, but after about September 1 no ferry trips are conducted on Tuesdays or Wednesdays. The ferry trips cost $2.00 (round trip) for adults. For senior citizens (age 62 and older) and children (age 15 and under) the cost is $1.00. No pets are permitted on the ferry or the island.

Reservations are required and should be made well in advance. Many visitors call or write as much as 60 days prior to their trip. Reservations may be made by writing Cumberland Island National Seashore, P.O. Box 806, St. Marys, GA 31558; or by telephoning the NPS office at (912)882-4335.

According to the park service personnel, few people miss the ferry returning to the mainland, since it means spending a night on the island without benefit of tent, sleeping bag or food. Some private boats can be chartered for the return trip, however, and the NPS rangers keep a list of phone numbers for this purpose. The cost is approximately $40 for the trip.

For day visitors, the NPS offers short walking tours of part of the island. Guides lead the way to the ruins of Dungeness mansion, explaining the island's history and pointing out flora and fauna along the way. After a short walk to the beach, visitors are returned to the boat dock for the ride back to St. Marys. These tours are conducted at 10:00 a.m. and 2:30 p.m. daily. Reservations are required and can be made at the same time ferry reservations are arranged.

There are no public facilities on Cumberland Island other

than comfort stations; drinking water is available. Visitors should bring their own food and dress appropriately for walking.

FISHING AND HUNTING: No hunting is permitted on Cumberland Island National Seashore.

Saltwater fishing can be good for channel bass, sea trout and bluefish on the ocean side. Anglers casting the western shore of Cumberland Island into Cumberland Sound may catch redfish, trout or croaker. No fishing licenses are required while fishing on the island.

Most surf anglers concentrate their efforts along the southern tip of the island where rock jetties extend out into the water along both sides of the St. Marys River channel. These jetties, built nearly a century ago to help break wave action for boats entering and leaving the channel, provide fine fishing action today. The jetties can be reached by walking to the beach from the Dungeness ruins, then southward along the dunes for approximately 1.5 miles.

WILDLIFE OBSERVATION: Cumberland Island abounds with wildlife, and even day visitors should see whitetail deer, squirrel, raccoon and probably wild turkey. Good spots to look for deer and turkey are along the edges of the island roads, the salt marshes and in the vicinity of the Dungeness mansion ruins.

During the spring and summer months, several species of birds nest on the island. The most noticeable are least terns, which lay their eggs on the sand dunes just out of reach of the high tides. Other birds that might be spotted here include egrets, ibises and several species of warblers.

Huge loggerhead turtles come ashore at night during the summer months to lay their eggs. Visitors rarely see these creatures and digging up or molesting their eggs is strictly forbidden. Because Cumberland is one of the few islands used by loggerheads, scientific study teams frequently patrol the beaches at night to help protect and mark the turtle nests.

CAMPING: Five camp areas are open on Cumberland Island—Sea Camp, Stafford Beach, Hickory Hill, Yankee Paradise and Brickhill Bluff. Reservations are required for

Backpackers walk along one of the shaded roads of Cumberland island. Visitors are not allowed to bring automobiles to this national seashore.

each area.

Sea Camp is the only "developed" campground, and it offers 16 sites for tents, rest rooms, showers and drinking water. Open campfires are permitted here as long as only dead-and-down wood is burned.

The other four camps are primitive areas with only drinking water available. Distances from these sites to dock at Sea Camp range from 3.5 to 10.5 miles. The only way to reach these camps is on foot.

Camping at present is limited to a total of 120 people per night, with a maximum of 60 at Sea Camp at any one time. After general camping reservations are made in advance, specific sites are assigned and backcountry-use permits issued upon arrival on Cumberland Island. All camping is free and limited to seven days. No fires are permitted in the primitive camp areas, and all trash must be packed out.

Expect your campsite to be visited by squirrels or raccoons, both of which will quickly get into food. Plan to hang your food from a tree limb, using the thinnest rope or line you can find. Squirrels will crawl down a rope, so some campers use strong fishing line to suspend their food bags.

HIKING: Hiking, especially in conjunction with backcountry camping, is the ideal way to discover the wonders of Cumberland Island. Nearly a dozen trails lace the full length of the island, leading the way to hidden lakes and seldom-visited marshes, or across the brilliant shifting sand dunes.

The major north-south route along the island is Grand Avenue, a one-land dirt road, and most of the trails branch off from it. The trails are marked by rustic wood signs and are maintained by park personnel. Over the dunes the trails are marked with directional arrows every few feet to insure that hikers do not stray off course.

The proper clothing for hiking, even on this island, includes heavy boots, long trousers and a hat. Mosquito repellent should be carried, and hikers should check frequently for ticks. Some poisonous snakes, such as diamondback rattlesnakes, may be encountered, so a snakebite kit is recommended.

The Cumberland Island National Seashore "Backcountry Map," available at the island visitor center, describes the various hiking trails and is free to backpackers and campers.

ADDITIONAL INFORMATION: Additional information is available by writing or telephoning the Cumberland Island National Seashore, P.O. Box 806, St. Marys, GA 31558; tel. (919) 882-4335.

The National Park Service has one colorful booklet for sale that describes this national seashore. Titled "Cumberland Island/A Place Apart," it is available for $1.50 from park headquarters in St. Marys.

The ruins of Dungeness, a short walk from the ferry dock, are just part of this island's fascinating history.

KENTUCKY

When exploring Daniel Boone's country, it is easy to see why the frontiersman liked it so much. Parts of the Daniel Boone National Forest still seem to look much the same as they did when Boone first saw them two centuries ago, with rolling timbered ridges, steep limestone cliffs and wind-and-water-sculptured rock arches. The history of Kentucky is woven closely with the life of Boone, for although he did not discover the famous Cumberland Gap, he did cut the first trail through it leading into Kentucky. Until that time, the Appalachian Mountains had been an impenetrable barrier to westward settlement. Within 20 years after Boone's trail blazing, more than 100,000 pioneers had moved into Kentucky.

Like many Southern states, Kentucky is hard at work constructing a network of hiking trails through the backcountry, and many, when completed, will follow Boone's footsteps.

Many of the wilderness activities take place in the national forest, which stretches from the Tennessee border near Middlesboro northward to Morehead. Cumberland Gap is located near the junction of Kentucky, Tennessee and Virginia. Major transportation arteries easily link all parts of the national forest with Lexington, Bowling Green and Louisville.

CUMBERLAND GAP NATIONAL HISTORIC PARK

"Following the Footsteps of Daniel Boone"

It is April 13, 1750, and explorer Thomas Walker of Albemarle County, Virginia, is standing on a low, sparsely wooded knoll with his five companions looking at a very prominent break in the mountain wall before them. It is a distinct gap, with a clear spring flowing on the north side, a well-used Indian trail on the south.

"This Gap may be seen at a considerable distance," Walker writes in his journal. "The Mountain on the North Side is very Steep and Rocky, but on the South it is not So. We called it Steep Ridge."

The "Steep Ridge" Walker named was Cumberland Gap, and on that spring day he and his party became the first white men to walk through it, to alter forever the history of America's westward expansion.

Colonial populations along the Atlantic coast had been halted in their movements by the steep Appalachian Mountains between Canada and Georgia. A few hunters and trappers had crossed the mountains before Walker, but the conditions were too harsh and dangerous for families and wagons to follow.

This natural break in the mountain wall had been in use for centuries by the Indians traveling along the famed Warriors' Path between the Ohio River to the north and the Carolinas to the south. Walker describes finding a "plain Indian Road" with trees cut with crosses and figures, and he himself reportedly carved his name on a beech tree nearby.

Walker was actually searching for the fabled Kentucky

bluegrass when he found Cumberland Gap, but it was not until 1752 that that fertile region was discovered by John Finley who had traveled down the Ohio to trade and hunt with the Shawnees. During these hunts Finley discovered that the Warriors' Path led all the way from southern Kentucky to Cumberland Gap.

The French and Indian War delayed any additional exploration, but by 1760 small hunting parties were again making their way into the region. In 1769 Daniel Boone crossed through the gap with Finley and four others. Harrassed and once even captured by the Shawnees, Boone spent the next two years in Kentucky, much of it hunting and traveling alone.

Within the next several years, treaties were signed with both the Shawnees and Cherokees, who subsequently surrendered their claims to the land of Kentucky and Cumberland Gap. Boone, with his thorough knowledge of the area, was hired to blaze a trail for settlers to follow across Cumberland Gap. He started on March 10, 1775, with about 30 men, felling trees and cutting a pathway between what is now Rose Hill, Virginia, through the gap to the mouth of Otter Creek on the Kentucky River. This was to become the famous Wilderness Road. At Otter Creek the party established the town of Boonesboro. Other small towns sprang up, and by 1790, just 15 years after Boone led the way, Kentucky's population had soared to nearly 75,000 people. What makes this figure astounding is that Boone cut only a foot trail, which was not suitably widened for wagon traffic until 1796.

Today U.S Highway 25E leads through Cumberland Gap following at least part of Boone's Wilderness Road, and over 20,000 acres have been set aside as Cumberland Gap National Historic Park, the largest park of its type in the system.

Atop one of the cliffs overlooking the gap is a rocky promontory named the Pinnacle, and from there it is possible to look out over the rolling Kentucky woodlands for miles. Much of the terrain looks unchanged from Boone's day, for there has been relatively little development in the park. Portions of some trails lead through incredibly thick stands of mountain laurel to the ridge line of Cumberland Mountain, or to the steep outcropping known as White Rocks—all things Boone saw and experienced in his explorations here. Unfortunately, the small museum in the Park Visitor Center does not have any of Boone's old possessions to make the region's history become even more alive.

Daniel Boone blazed the first trail through Cumberland Gap for settlers to follow. Today hikers can follow Boone's footsteps through the gap and over the high ridges he explored over two centuries ago.

Wilderness Road Trail

Historical Pass 5 mi 1 k

One place where history does come alive is at Hensley Settlement, a pioneer community that was born in 1903, died in 1951 and is being restored by the National Park Service. Today it is a living historical farm, operated by people who work and live there much as the Hensley family did. The settlement can be reached only by trails or by four-wheel drive vehicle.

According to rangers, the park receives relatively light use. A system of trails leads through the backcountry to offer a fine wilderness experience for those who enjoy combining history with hiking. Seldom is one far from the sights and sounds of modern civilization here and wildlife is not often seen, but with just a little imagination, it is easy to believe Boone and Finley and Walker are just around the next bend on the trail.

HOW TO VISIT CUMBERLAND GAP

Cumberland Gap is not hard to locate. Just pick up any map that includes the states of Virginia, Tennessee and Kentucky. Less than 400 yards from where these three states meet is Cumberland Gap. The nearest city is Middlesboro, Kentucky, where Cumberland Gap National Historic Park Headquarters is located.

If you are heading north or south through this part of the country, you will have to go right through the gap, for it is still the only pass through the Cumberland Mountains for miles in either direction. The highway is U.S. 25E from Morristown, Tennessee, to Corbin, Kentucky.

The first stop in the park should be at the headquarters building, approximately two miles north of the gap on U.S. 25E. A ten-minute slide presentation details some of Cumberland Gap's colorful history and helps acquaint visitors with the region. Backcountry-use permits are required for trail camping, and they can be picked up here.

For beautiful views of the mountains the settlers had to cross, plan to drive north along U.S. 58 between Cumberland Gap and Ewing through the area known as Powell Valley.

HIKING AND BACKPACKING: Walking is definitely the best way to explore this park and to get some feeling for what Boone and the early settlers experienced. Nearly all the longer overnight trails involve some fairly steep climbing, for they lead to the summit ridge of Cumberland Mountain and along its crest for several miles. The longest trail is the Ridge Trail, a 16-miler following this crest the entire length of the backcountry. It dips and climbs along the Virginia-Kentucky boundary and offers spectacular views of the region. This trail actually begins at the Pinnacle, a high rocky overlook which may be reached by automobile, and continues to Hensley Settlement, Sand Cave and White Rocks, prominent landmarks noted by Boone.

Several shorter trails have been constructed, and several loop trips are possible. The Woodson Gap Trail leads from the Wilderness Road Campground about three miles to the Ridge Trail atop Cumberland Mountain; and the Lewis Hollow Trail leads from the Wilderness Road Picnic Area for just over a mile up to the Ridge Trail to make a nice six-mile hike. The Gibson Gap Trail is a longer route up to the Ridge Trail, winding for about five miles from the Wilderness Road Campground to the mountaintop. Other shorter but steeper trails leading to the Ridge Trail are the Chadwell Gap Trail and the Ewing Trail, which take the hiker near Hensley Settlement and Sand Cave, respectively.

Backpackers should plan to purchase the helpful booklet "Why Not Walk?" at park headquarters when getting backcountry-use permits. This publication briefly describes the park trails, provides topographic map coverage of each and also includes an important section on park rules.

CAMPING: There are four campgrounds in Cumberland Gap National Historic Park, three of which can be reached only by hiking. These three are free of charge, but backcountry-use permits are required; the permit also serves as a campsite reservation for backpackers. The backcountry campgrounds are Gibson Gap, Martins Fork and White Rocks. Gibson Gap can accommodate up to 30 people, Martins Fork holds 75, and White Rocks takes 40 campers. Martins Fork does include a small unfurnished cabin for overnight use, available by reservation only.

Water may or may not be available at these campsites, and should be purified when it is. Gibson Gap and White Rocks campgrounds are often without water during the summer. Campfires are permitted with dead-and-down wood, but pack stoves are recommended. No dogs are allowed on the trails.

The Wilderness Road Campground has been developed for auto and RV campers and includes water and restrooms, pic-

In his explorations Daniel Boone used white rocks as a major landmark near the Cumberland Gap. Today backpackers can hike to the steep cliffs and follow along the ridge line to Cumberland Gap along the well-marked Ridge Trail.

nic tables and cooking grills. There are no showers or electrical hookups. The cost per night is $2.00 per site. The campground offers approximately 160 sites and is a good starting point for backcountry treks, since several trails begin here.

FISHING AND HUNTING: No hunting is permitted in Cumberland Gap National Historic Park.

There is some fishing available in Shillalah Creek and Martins Fork for brook trout. The season usually runs from May 15 to September 15; only artificial flies or single hook lures may be used. The limit is two trout over 12-inches. A Kentucky fishing license and trout stamp are required.

For additional information, contact the Department of Fish and Wildlife Resources, 592 East Main Street, Frankfort, KY 40601.

WILDLIFE OBSERVATION: Although several species of mammals and reptiles inhabit the park, most are rarely seen, even by the backcountry camper. Deer are occasionally spotted along the ridge of Cumberland Mountain, as are rabbit, squirrel and raccoon. Fox and bobcat are rarely encountered.

More than 125 species of birds have been identified in the park, and many can be sighted along the various trails. In the fall, hawks and other raptores follow the warm air thermals down the ridge of Cumberland Mountain in their southern migrations.

ADDITIONAL INFORMATION: For additional information, contact the Superintendent, Cumberland Gap National Historic Park, P.O. Box 840, Middlesboro, KY 40965.

BEAVER CREEK WILDERNESS
"Boone's Garden of Eden"

Much of nature's most dramatic handiwork is in stone, where wind and water have formed natural bridges, steep-walled cliffs and plunging waterfalls. There are few places in the south where such creations occur together in any great numbers, but one such area is the Daniel Boone National Forest of Kentucky. Right in the middle of this forest is the 5,000-acre Beaver Creek Wilderness, embracing the three scenic and rugged forks of Beaver Creek. The wilderness is contained within the Beaver Creek Wildlife Management Area where all development has been halted, so wilderness lovers have over 16,000 acres in which to roam.

Although there are no arches or stone bridges within the actual Beaver Creek boundaries, there are plenty of sheer cliffs, clear-splashing streams and big trees. The arches are but a short distance away, and throughout the region there are several dozen of them.

This is Daniel Boone's old hunting territory, a land he is said to have described as Eden, with "trees 10 feet in diameter and 150 feet tall." Few of those big trees are still here, but Beaver Creek does have the Kentucky record yellow poplar that might have been growing when the famous frontiersman walked this country.

Before Boone's explorations, southern Kentucky was inhabited by several Indian tribes, primarily the Shawnees and Cherokees. Many of them lived in the region's shallow caves or under the overhanging cliffs, known locally as rock houses. Buffalo, deer and other game were abundant. Gradually, as settlers came in, the land was cleared along the ridges and

83

Standing at the Forest Service overlook on the Three Forks of Beaver Trail, a hiker looks at the deep canyons and dark forests of the Beaver Creek Wilderness. Here, the three forks of Beaver Creek join before flowing into the Cumberland River.

small towns were constructed. Timber and coal became major industries, and much of today's Beaver Creek Wilderness was cut. These activities came to an end about 1910, and gradually the area towns were abandoned. In the 1930s the land was acquired by the U.S. Forest Service.

Man's impact has been heavy on Beaver Creek, for various roads crisscross the wilderness, and the ruins of abandoned mines, tunnels and homesteads can still be seen by backpackers. Modern-day strip-mining activities nearby once threatened to pollute Beaver Creek, for this region is rich in coal deposits; that threat may appear again in the future.

Geologically, Beaver Creek is part of the Cumberland Plateau, an area of rolling hills, long ridges and deep, narrow gorges. Several dozen stone bridges and arches dot the canyons both north and south of Beaver Creek, and the streams are characterized by steep falls and ledges. Cumberland Falls, Yahoo Falls and Princess Falls—Kentucky's best known waterfalls—are just a few miles from the wilderness.

Beaver Creek contains a wide variety of trees and plants, and botanists have identified 13 separate forest cover types here.

Oak and hickory thrive along the higher, drier ridges, while poplar, hemlock and maple have grown tall and heavy in the lower hollows and canyons. A walk along the overlook trail leads through several of these forest types, which are quite noticeable even to the most casual observer. Closer to the ground ginseng, filmy fern, and goldenseal, all rare and endangered plants, may be found.

Several species of wild game, present when Boone traveled through Kentucky, are still found in the Beaver Creek watershed. Whitetail deer and wild turkey prowl the hardwood ridges, while in the trees above a small colony of endangered red-cockaded woodpeckers is reported to be holding its own. Copperheads and timber rattlers might be seen warming themselves on sunny rocks, ruffed grouse whirr through the timber with their bursting speed, and gray and red foxes slip quietly along the stream banks in the dawn.

Because there are few trails in the Beaver Creek Wilderness, today's backpacker has the opportunity to return briefly to the ways of Boone and the other explorers, setting his own course across the ridges and down the canyons. It is worth trying.

Nearby Cumberland Falls is one of only two waterfalls in the world that have moonbows—rainbows that shine by moonlight; the other waterfall is Victoria Falls in South Africa. The moonbow is visible only a few nights each month during the full moon.

HOW TO VISIT BEAVER CREEK WILDERNESS

Like many national forest wilderness areas, the Beaver Creek Wilderness is easy to get to, but it is hard to tell when you are actually there. Signs are few and far between, as vandals continually tear markers down to use as souvenirs. The wilderness is contained entirely within the 16,500-acre Beaver Creek Wildlife Management Area, and signs marking its boundaries are very prominent, so when you see one of them you know you are getting close.

Beaver Creek Wilderness is located in McCreary County in the southern portion of the Daniel Boone National Forest, south of Somerset and west of Corbin. U.S. Highway 27 and Ky. Highway 90 from the western and southern area boundaries. The actual wilderness boundary lines generally follow the ridges of the three forks of Beaver Creek.

A number of logging roads provide some access into the Wilderness, but these are not well marked. The easiest entry is near milepost 22 on U.S. 27, turning east on the paved road (Forest Service Road 50) leading to Hammons Camp on Lake Cumberland. Follow this road for two miles and turn right on the first gravel road, FS511, which leads to a small parking lot and the trailhead for Three Forks of Beaver Trail overlook.

HIKING AND BACKPACKING: Established trails in the Beaver Creek Wilderness presently consist only of short loop trails less than two miles in length. Backpackers can follow the different forks of Beaver Creek or hike along the various ridges, but travel will be difficult. The cliffs are extremely steep, and high water conditions will force hikers away from the rocky stream beds.

The trail to the Beaver Creek overlook begins at the gravel parking lot off FS 511 and winds for a mile or so through various forest types to a rocky pinnacle overlooking the wilderness. This trail is well marked, easy to follow and not strenuous.

A hike along FS 51 can be a pleasant experience, for the road generally follows the ridge line above Beaver Creek and then drops down to the creek. Here another hike is possible up Beaver Creek as far as one feels like traveling.

Backpackers in the Beaver Creek Wilderness walk through a carpet of leaves during the fall. Hikers normally follow the streams, since there are few established hiking trails in the wilderness.   Photo by U.S. Forest Service

No backcountry-use permits are required, and camping is allowed throughout the wilderness. No dogs are allowed.

A longer backpacking trail that winds through much of the Daniel Boone National Forest but which actually by-passes the Beaver Creek Wilderness is the Sheltowee Trace National Recreation Trail, which, when completed, will extend from Pickett State Park, Tennessee, to the Pioneer Weapons Hunting Area, a distance of nearly 250 miles. The trail was named for Daniel Boone, who was given the name Sheltowee (meaning Big Turtle) when he was adopted into the Shawnee tribe. Additional information on the open sections of the trail is available from the Supervisor's Office, Daniel Boone National Forest.

CAMPING: Backcountry camping in the Beaver Creek Wilderness is permitted anywhere a hiker wants to pitch a tent. The ridgetops provide the best sites, for the ground is level, soft and drains well.

Other established campgrounds nearby in the national forest include Little Lick and Alum Ford recreation areas and several spots along the shoreline of Laurel River Lake. Camping is limited at Cumberland Falls State Park, but very good sites are available a few miles east of the park on Ky. 90 at Raines Travel Trailer Park and Campground.

HUNTING AND FISHING: The Beaver Creek Wildlife Management Area remains closed to all hunting activity. Much of the national forest hunting takes place in the Pioneer Weapons Hunting Area north of the wilderness. Only pioneer-type weapons may be used, as hunters test their skills against deer, turkey, squirrel, grouse and quail.

In years past trout were stocked in Beaver Creek, but this practice has been stopped. The best fishing opportunities are in nearby Laurel River Lake, Cave Run Lake, Lake Cumberland and Licking and Kentucky rivers. Rock Creek and Bark Camp Creek offer good trout fishing. Cave Run Lake has gained a national reputation for its muskie population, and Lake Cumberland for its bass, crappie and walleye.

For additional information, contact the Department of Fish and Wildlife Resources, 592 East Main Street, Frankfort, KY 40601.

RAFTING AND CANOEING: Commercial rafting trips down the Cumberland River Gorge below Cumberland Falls are offered daily between May and October. The trips last about four hours, and all safety equipment is provided. The cost is approximately $20.00 per person.

Portions of the upper Red River and the Big South Fork of the Cumberland River have been designated as Kentucky Wild Rivers and provide plenty of thrills for white-water canoeists and kayakers. The lower Red River and upper Cumberland offer more leisurely trips on quiet waters.

For additional information, contact Cumberland Outdoor Adventures, Route 6, Box 410A, Corbin, KY 40701.

WILDLIFE OBSERVATION: Whitetail deer are the primary game animals of this region, with backpackers possibly seeing squirrel, turkey, ruffed grouse or fox. This is largely vertical country with steep cliffs and drops, and most game will either be on the upper ridges or in the creek canyons below.

Daniel Boone described the area as having an "abundance of wild beasts of all sorts" and with "buffalo more frequent than cattle in the settlements." Today a visitor to the region can search for over 40 different species of mammals and more than 100 species of birds.

ADDITIONAL INFORMATION: For additional information and free brochures describing the Beaver Creek Wilderness and the national forest, write the District Ranger, U.S. Forest Service, Rte. 2, Box 507, Somerset, KY 42501; or the Supervisor, Daniel Boone National Forest, 100 Vaught Road, Winchester, KY 40391.

LOUISIANA

The Bayou State cannot boast of any rugged mountains or rolling white-water rivers, but it does have wild terrain. The Atchafalaya Basin is a region roughly 18 miles wide and over 100 miles long located in the southern portion of the state between Lafayette and Baton Rouge and extending to the Gulf. For quiet, backwater canoeing through a world of towering cypress and flashing warblers, the Atchafalaya is the South's best.

Backpackers and campers can also enjoy the 595,000-acre Kisatchie National Forest, which includes the Kisatchie Hills, sandstone formations left over from eons past.

Because of these two major recreation areas, shops and stores in metropolitan areas like Baton Rouge, Lafayette and Shreveport are well stocked to cater to packers and paddlers. Canoe rentals are available in several cities, and guided trips are possible.

Abundant wildlife ranges throughout both the Atchafalaya and Kisatchie, including deer, alligator, turkey, numerous species of birds and several varieties of poisonous snakes. The summer months are probably the most uncomfortable for extended outdoor activities due to heat and humidity, and spring usually signals high water in the Atchafalaya from northern melted snow. Fall is pleasant, and winter is normally mild.

THE ATCHAFALAYA BASIN
"Where the Water and the Willows Meet"

It is noontime on a warm spring day in southern Louisiana, and Joe Boutin pauses briefly in his paddling to dip a handful of cool water and splash it over his face. Then he begins again, guiding the tiny wooden pirogue across the bayou and into a narrow, cypress-lined creek. Soon it is too shallow for even the pirogue, and Boutin steps out into the mud and continues on foot, pulling the narrow boat behind him.

He continues wading, but soon he is no longer alone. Dark shadows flash through the trees, and the air is filled with raucous shrieks and cries. Boutin has reached his destination: a heron rookery deep in a hidden niche of the Atchafalaya Basin.

Practically every cypress for 50 yards around has a nest of black-crowned night herons, white egrets or anhingas, and limbs sag from the weight. The nests themselves look like no more than piles of sticks and twigs balanced precariously between the branches, but small fuzzy heads and chirping beaks peer out from most of them.

For the next two hours Boutin will sit silently in his pirogue watching the spectacle. He does not take pictures, make official bird counts or tag nests. He just sits and watches quietly, because he enjoys it.

"To me, this is what the Atchafalaya is all about," he says. "You have to get back into its hidden corners to really understand and appreciate what this place is all about."

The Atchafalaya Basin is many things to many different

people. Eighteen miles wide, 130 miles long, stretching roughly from Simmesport, Louisiana, to the Gulf of Mexico, it is America's largest remaining forested wetland wilderness. Although timber hunters removed a fortune in cypress from the swamp half a century ago, second-growth trees form a watery jungle that is home for hundreds of species of birds and mammals. Deer and black bear prowl through the basin's interior, and many ornithologists believe the fabled ivory-billed woodpecker may still live here.

This vast water-and-cypress world is the center of Louisiana's $47 million crawfish industry. For several months each year, Cajun crawfishermen set their wire mesh traps throughout the swamp, checking them daily from dawn to dusk and bringing their catch back to shore packed tightly in 50-pound sacks. Crawfish can only be successfully taken during periods of high water in the spring, and because of this short season, a crawfisherman may set out as many as 400 traps. He sells the crawfish for between $.30 and $1.00 a pound to buyers right on the boat landings.

The Atchafalaya Basin is also a gigantic flood control safety valve for the Mississippi River. Water from 31 states and two Canadian provinces eventually flows into the Mississippi River. At Simmesport, part of this water is funneled into the Atchafalaya River where it floods the wetlands as part of an ageless cycle of nature making the basin the rich biological wonderland that it is.

Because man has altered nature's ways by channelizing other rivers and clearing the land of trees to farm, the Atchafalaya is changing. It is gradually filling with silt caused by increased water runoff from midwestern states. Though slow siltation is a natural process, in the Atchafalaya it is occurring faster than normal. This siltation is raising the water level throughout the basin, creating islands, burying lakes and forming the growing base for weeping willows.

These processes have caused a direct confrontation between ecologists and engineers over the eventual fate of the Atchafalaya. Some engineers believe dredging the main channel of the Atchafalaya River is necessary to increase the water flow and carry the silt to the Gulf. This would, however, lower the basin's actual water level in the swamp marshes, which would be disastrous to the crawfish industry, to sport fishing and to the wildlife population as well.

Another factor plays a part in the controversy. The majority of the Atchafalaya is privately owned; about 80 percent of the entire basin is owned by just four individuals and seven companies. Right now, these landowners are getting little or no financial return on their holdings. Lowering the Atchafalaya's water level would make more of the land accessible to them. Once the cypress trees were removed, the ground could be plowed and planted with soybeans, for it is some of the richest earth in America.

The Atchafalaya's problems actually date to 1927, when the Mississippi River flooded from an extremely heavy snow melt and spring rains. The Atchafalaya flooded with it. The next year, the U.S. Congress passed the Flood Control Act for the Atchafalaya Basin, committing the U.S. Army Corps of Engineers to a flood control program that would save New Orleans and other Louisiana cities from any more disastrous floods in the future.

The Corps began dredging the northern portion of the Atchafalaya Basin, constructing high levees on both riverbanks to control high water. This allowed water to flow more rapidly through the upper section of the Atchafalaya, but upon reaching the basin's shallower lower end, the water slowed down. As it slowed silt was deposited, filling in several lakes and forming new sand bars where willows quickly sprang up.

In 1950 the Atchafalaya flooded again, and in 1954 the Corps began dredging operations in the lower basin. This continued for 14 years until funds for the work were exhausted. By this time a number of area residents had already begun to notice changes in the swamp. The high water overflow so necessary to the overall survival of the basin's wildlife was being halted.

In 1969 Congress passed the National Environmental Policy Act requiring that environmental impact statements be made whenever an area's ecological balance is threatened by technical progress. By 1974 the preliminary impact statement had been completed and a concept for Atchafalaya management formulated. A multi-purpose plan that will take years to fully implement, it involves the purchase of easements across the private land and construction of special flood control structures that will allow the Atchafalaya to flood, despite deep water channelization.

Even with these foreboding problems, the Atchafalaya is still an enchanting place to visit. The area abounds with old-timers who grew up in the swamp and made their living cutting cypress or trapping crawfish. Some continue to live in the swamp itself, although most have now moved to neighboring towns.

Earlis Carline, now 66, resides in a small cabin he built years ago as part of his Atchafalaya homestead. His wife and children live in town, and he commutes weekly by boat to see them. The main channel of the Atchafalaya laps at his doorstep; the green walls of the swamp form a solid curtain behind his cabin. He did some fur trapping in his younger days, and crawfishing too. He remembers a place called Grand Lake, located south of his cabin, which was silted in by the river's fast flow.

"This is home," he told a boatload of visitors, "no matter what happens to the Atchafalaya, and I'll stay here as long as I can. Changes have come here just like every place else, and the Atchafalaya's not through changing yet, and I'll just wait right here and watch as it happens."

Most of the big cypress was logged out of the Atchafalaya many years ago, but some giants still remain, trees that were not cut because of deformities in the wood.   Photo by Charles Fryling, Jr.

HOW TO VISIT THE ATCHAFALAYA

It is not that difficult to venture into the Atchafalaya Basin to see the cypress forest and its wildlife. Visitors can get a glimpse of the basin from Interstate 10 between Baton Rouge and Lafayette without ever leaving their automobiles. This portion of the expressway crosses the Atchafalaya completely and has exits at Whiskey Bay and Butte La Rose landings. From Whiskey Bay it is possible to travel along the top of the eastern levee to Krotz Springs and U.S. Highway 190, which crosses the Atchafalaya from Baton Rouge. From Krotz Springs, it is also possible to travel southward on the western levee to Butte La Rose.

Interstate 10 continues across one of the Atchafalaya's largest lakes, Lake Henderson, which gives the visitor some idea of the appearance of the swamp's many hidden fishing holes. Just west of Lake Henderson one can exit the expressway on LA. Highway 347, cutting back to Henderson. From the swamp levee road it is possible to drive northward or southward for miles along the Atchafalaya's western boundary. It is also possible to see the eastern edge of the Atchafalaya, traveling northward from Morgan City off U.S. 90; or southward from Ramah Landing off I-10.

Visitors will find several boat launching areas, such as Henderson Landing, Doucet Landing, Catahoula Landing, Bayou Benoit Landing and others. Crawfishermen, sport and commercial anglers and boat tours leave from these launches to the Atchafalaya's interior.

CANOEING AND RAFTING: Canoe or small motorboat is by far the best way to explore the vast Atchafalaya Basin wilderness, expecially when in the company of an experienced guide who knows the area. It is possible to put in at many of the landings mentioned above and paddle or motor down various creeks and bayous in a long loop trip, or come out at a different landing. Most of the creeks are narrow and winding, providing easy scenic paddling. Canoeing the main channel of the Atchafalaya is not recommended due to fast current and barge traffic.

Outdoor shops which offer canoe rentals and guided trips are: Canoe and Trail Shop, 624 Moss Street, New Orleans, LA 70112; Pack and Paddle, 601 Pinhook Road East, Lafayette,

LA 70503; and The Backpacker, 3378 Highland Road Mall, Baton Rouge, LA 70802.

Dr. Charles Fryling, a professor in the school of Environmental Design of Louisiana State University in Baton Rouge, has been exploring the Atchafalaya for 12 years by canoe and frequently leads trips into the interior. Occasionally it is possible to accompany him on such trips. He may be contacted at 1068 East Lakeview Drive, Baton Rouge, LA 70810.

Do not attempt to venture into the Atchafalaya without a guide on your first visit to the swamp. To a newcomer many of the winding creeks and channels look alike, and it is easy to become disoriented.

FISHING AND HUNTING: Because most of the land itself is privately owned, hunting is largely controlled by various clubs how have leased hunting rights. The basin harbors large populations of deer and turkey, as well as the largest gathering of wintering woodcock in the United States. Hunting information can be furnished by the Louisiana Department of Wildlife and Fisheries, 400 Royal Street, New Orleans, LA 70130.

Sport fishing is excellent in the basin for largemouth bass, crappie (known locally as sac-a-lait) and catfish. The best fishing occurs after the high water conditions have receded in late spring, pulling the fish out of the flooded woodlands and into the canals and bayous. Places like Lost Lake, Cow Island Lake and other spots regularly produce a heavy stringer of largemouth bass; water may be clear in these lakes even though high and muddy in other areas. Acre for acre, the Atchafalaya produces more fish than any other natural water system in the United States.

There are few, if any, regular fishing guides for the Atchafalaya. If you want to try your luck, inquire at one of the many boat landings along the levees or contact the Louisiana Department of Wildlife and Fisheries (address above).

WILDLIFE OBSERVATION: To see the Atchafalaya's wildlife, it is necessary to venture into the basin itself. Deer frequent the higher, drier land in the northern portion, while birds and alligators are more commonly seen in the lower areas. Wild turkey, black bear, bobcat and fox are rarely seen, although substantial populations exist in the Atchafalaya.

There are no regularly conducted wildlife observation tours in the Atchafalaya. The best way to observe or photograph the region's animal life is to travel with a local guide by canoe or pirogue, or on foot. The canoe trip outfitters (addresses given above) can also provide help in arranging wildlife trips.

Over 300 species of birds have been identified in the Atchafalaya, including the bald eagle. Over 50,000 egrets, ibises and herons nest here, and in winter the water is alive with migrating waterfowl. Although many species may be seen while traveling along the levees, the best opportunities for bird observation are by boat.

CAMPING: There is no camping in the Atchafalaya, since most of the land is private and no campgrounds presently exist.

HIKING: Hiking is best along the Atchafalaya's levees, although these routes do not provide much of an opportunity to really study the swamp. The Atchafalaya is primarily a watery world. If you do plan to hike, walk northward along the levee from Whiskey Bay Landing.

ADDITIONAL INFORMATION: Additional information on the Atchafalaya Basin may be obtained from Dr. Charles Fryling, Jr., 1068 East Lakeview Drive, Baton Rouge, LA 70810; the U.S. Army Corps of Engineers, New Orleans District, Box 60267, Attn: LMNPDA-A, New Orleans, LA 70160; U.S. Fish and Wildlife Service, 111 East Main Street, Lafayette, LA 70501; and the Louisiana Wildlife Federation, P.O. Box 16089 LSU, Baton Rouge, LA 70893.

Maps of the Atchafalaya Basin are available free from the Office of State Parks, P.O. Drawer 1111, Baton Rouge, LA 70821.

An American egret stalks the shallows in search of a meal. The Atchafalaya is incredibly rich in fish life and is the heart of Louisiana's huge crawfish industry.

NORTH CAROLINA

From the summit of the highest mountain in eastern North America, Mount Mitchell, to the pocosin lowlands of the coast, North Carolina offers a seldom-matched variety of outdoor recreation for lovers of wild places. A good bit of the western portion of the Tarheel State is covered by the Pisgah and Nantahala national forests, Great Smoky Mountains National Park and the Blue Ridge Mountains. Backpackers can follow the same trails the early settlers used two centuries ago to carve their homesteads into these forests.

On the southern coast between New Bern and Morehead City, a totally different type of environment exists in the Croatan National Forest, one in which the land is organically rich but high in acidity and low in nutrients. It is called *pocosin,* a word signifying a raised bog where shrubs and vines are stunted and trees are usually absent.

In addition to these two forested areas, the state's rivers provide everything from the waves and drops of the Nantahala to the slow, jungle-like atmosphere of the Waccamaw.

The state is well aware of its outdoor attractions and has an active staff in its travel and promotion offices in Raleigh to help visitors plan trips. Travel throughout North Carolina is extremely easy and efficient, both by automobile or by air.

LINVILLE GORGE WILDERNESS
"Pisgah's Roughest Place"

High on the slopes of famous Grandfather Mountain north of Morganton, North Carolina, several tiny springs and sparkling runoff creeks join forces to form the Linville River, one of the state's most turbulent white-water streams. In its wild run through the mountains to the broad Catawba Valley, the river has churned a deep, twisting 12-mile canyon known as Linville Gorge, and Congress has protected it as the 7600-acre Linville Gorge Wilderness.

Embraced by the steep cliffs of Linville Mountain on one side and Jonas Ridge on the other, the river drops over 2000 feet in elevation through the gorge, creating a continuous roar clearly audible from the ridges above. It is a fine trout river, and some people also attempt to float it with rafts, but the major attraction of Linville Gorge is its rugged backpacking.

Several winding trails lead down to the river to meet the Linville Gorge Trail, which follows the water its entire length through the canyon. Several of the trails are steep, for the summit ridges rise abruptly for 600 feet or more in places, and Laurel Knob, the highest point on Linville Mountain, is more than 1640 feet above the river.

Nature and time have done their handiwork well in Linville Gorge. Jonas Ridge looks like a sculptor's workshop with its massive boulders, ledges, spires and fissures. Some of these formations have been named Table Rock, Hawksbill, Sitting Bear and the Chimneys for the things they resemble.

Plant life is as diversified as the rock formations in this wilderness, and backpackers will walk through a garden of mountain laurel, rhododendron, chokeberry, yellowroot and

100

alder. In places, because the growing space is so slight, plants have sprouted from the rocks themselves. There are portions of virgin forest withint the gorge, since the early lumberjacks had no way of getting logs to sawmills. Trails lead through a mixture of oak and pine, ash, maple, locust and holly.

The area has been known as a plant wonderland for many years. As early as 1802 French botanist Andre Michaux visited the gorge while on a collecting trip for his government. Both the gorge and the river were named for explorer William Linville, who with his son was scalped by Indians here in 1766.

The gorge actually begins approximately 0.5 mile north of the wilderness boundary at beautiful Linville Falls, a double waterfall easily reached by visitors along a short trail through the forest. There are no other falls of this magnitude within the wilderness. There are, however, numerous smaller waterfalls plunging into deep pools where an angler might tempt a wily rainbow or brown trout.

Rock climbers will also enjoy the rugged wonders of this wilderness, practicing their sport along the challenging sections of Hawksbill and the Chimneys of Jonas Ridge. Beginner, intermediate and advanced rock specialists all have their choice of dozens of different routes available.

As a testimony to its rugged terrain and lack of accessibility, Linville Gorge was among the first wilderness areas designated by Congress in 1964. It is a part of the Pisgah National Forest and is within a day's drive of a large portion of the nation's population. As a result of heavy use, a permit system has been initiated by Forest Service personnel to help preserve the area's wild flavor.

From Wiseman's View visitors may see Linville Gorge and the rugged cliffs embracing it.

HOW TO VISIT LINVILLE GORGE

Linville Gorge is considered one of the most rugged but scenic canyons in the South. The trails leading down to the Linville River and the Linville Gorge Trail following the river are generally easy to follow, but in the case of any accidents, help is a long distance away.

The Linville Gorge Wilderness Area is near the town of Linville Falls, approximately 20 miles north of Marion, North Carolina, via U.S. Highway 221. One of the major attractions in the region is Linville Falls at the head of the gorge, but the actual wilderness boundary is about half a mile south.

It is possible to see part of Linville Gorge by following N.C. Highway 183 out of Linville Falls and turning south on old N.C. 105. This road leads to the waterfall parking lot and continues along the ridge of Linville Mountain. The various trails leading into the gorge have their trailheads along this road. One overlook at Wiseman's View provides an excellent panorama of the gorge and surrounding wilderness.

CAMPING: Camping is permitted anywhere in the gorge, but most campers stay near the river due to the steep walls of the canyon. Permits are required, and camping is limited to a maximum of three days and two nights. Weekends are crowded, through not with campers since only 30 overnight permits are issued at once, but with day visitors who walk the trails down to the water.

Forest Service personnel do not recommend drinking Linville River water unless it is purified beforehand. Bugs and mosquitoes are not a major problem. Poisonous snakes may be encountered, but the greatest hazard is probably sprained ankles caused by falls or slips. Plan to do your cooking on a portable stove, and pack out all garbage.

HIKING AND BACKPACKING: Much has changed since Linville Gorge was declared a wilderness in 1964. Permits are required of everyone who plans to visit the gorge, and they are only issued 30 days or more in advance. Backpackers are limited to two nights and three days in the canyon, and no more than 30 persons are allowed in overnight at once. A maximum of 100 day-use permits are issued daily. Permits are issued by the U.S. Forest Service District Office in Marion (address below), and at the Country Store located on U.S. 221 north of the town of Linville Falls.

In the fall of 1978, forestry personnel completed the Linville Gorge Trail, which runs along the river for the entire length of the wilderness, a distance of around ten miles. Several access trails lead to this trail from both canyon rims. On the west side these trails are Pine Gap, Bynum Bluff, Cabin, Babel Tower, Sandy Flats, Conley Cove and Pinch In. Along the eastern side, Devil's Hole and Spence Ridge trails lead to the river. Several of these trails are considered primitive and are extremely steep but well marked. To hike the full length of the wilderness, one should plan to reach the river via the Pine Gap Trail, then follow the Linville Gorge Trail down to the Pinch In Trail and

Trout fishing for both rainbows and browns is popular in Linville Gorge, with numerous deep pools below rapids and falls.

hike out there. This is a long trip for the time limit allowed in the gorge, but it can be done.

CANOEING AND RAFTING: Neither canoeing nor rafting is recommended for the Linville River, because in its flow down the gorge the river drops more than 2000 feet. The water is filled with boulders, log jams and waterfalls. These sports are not forbidden by the U.S. Forest Service, however, and some rafting is done on the river. Backcountry-use permits are required.

FISHING AND HUNTING: Hunting is permitted in the wilderness during season for deer, bear, grouse, squirrel and raccoon. Bear is probably the most sought-after game animal in the area, but few are taken.

Fishing is popular in the Linville River, and anglers may try for rainbow and brown trout in the upper reaches of the Linville River and through most of the gorge. Bass are found in the water above Lake James. Fly fishing is especially popular.

For additional information on hunting and fishing regulations, contact the North Carolina Wildlife Resources Commission, 512 North Salisbury, Raleigh, NC 27611.

WILDLIFE OBSERVATION: Bear, deer, raccoon and squirrel all call the Linville Gorge Wilderness home, but only squirrel are seen regularly by backpackers and campers. Deer might be spotted coming to the river for an evening drink, but bear rarely will be seen.

ADDITIONAL INFORMATION: Information and permits may be obtained by contacting the District Ranger, U.S. Forest Service, P.O. Box 519, Marion, NC 28752. Permits are issued 30 days or more in advance, and may be obtained free of charge by writing.

SHINING ROCK WILDERNESS
"Climbing to the Top of the Smokies"

The brochure reads, "Wilderness, Do Not Enter . . . unless you are seeking the sounds of tumbling streams, the taste of clean air, and a slice of solitude . . ." It is a fitting introduction to North Carolina's 13,600-acre Shining Rock Wilderness in Pisgah National Forest. Here, atop the high ridges of the Smokies, the land looks as it has for centuries, with the same waterfalls, steep-sided cliffs and panoramas the Indians and early settlers first enjoyed.

The "shining rocks" are several huge chunks of quartz outcropping on the summit of 6000-foot Shining Rock Mountain. Volcanic action in the region produced these formations, and erosion has exposed them so that they glisten brightly under a summer sun.

In early summer, two other colors dominate the region — pink and purple — produced by the flowering rhododendron and mountain laurel. The wilderness supports five different rhododendrons and two species of mountain laurel, which often grow in thick jungles 20 to 30 feet tall. The forests are a mixture of spruce, fir and hemlock, evergreens of the Canadian vegetation zone but common in this part of the Smokies.

Two of the more interesting evergreens here are Fraser's fir, which is known locally as "she balsam," and red spruce, called "he balsam." Maybe the distinctions arise because the fir has cones projecting upward, while the spruce cones point downward. Both are popular Christmas trees.

Here, as in other parts of these mountains, there are also many large open meadows, the result of early logging activities as well as past forest fires. Much of what is now the Pisgah National Forest was once part of the vast George Vanderbilt Biltmore Estate. America's first school of forestry began in these woods in 1898, and restored buildings from the school are located just south of the wilderness on U.S. Highway 276. In the 1920s the land was transferred to the U.S. Forest Service with wilderness status granted in 1964.

Clear, splashing streams lace the wilderness, and the Pigeon River originates here. Because of the rugged up-and-down topography, there are numerous waterfalls throughout the wilderness, and several backpacking trails have wet crossings. Deep pools punctuate the rapids and falls, offering anglers fine opportunities for rainbow or brook trout.

The only way to get the full feeling of this wilderness area is on foot, and that means climbing. Elevations vary from about 3500 feet to over 6000 feet on the summit of Cold Mountain, and many of the trails climb to the summit ridges from the valleys below. There are about 25 miles of trails crossing the wilderness, with most leading eventually to the Shining Rocks.

Even in summer campers and hikers will find the higher elevations refreshingly cool, and frost may cover a tent or sleeping

Backpackers will find wet crossings along some of the trails, and in spring such crossings may be particularly hazardous because of high water conditions.

A trio of hikers looks over a trail map prior to starting into the wilderness. Trails here are generally well marked but most are steep.

bag in mid-June. In fall the lower elevations will be painted with the bright oranges, golds and reds of changing leaves, and in winter snow will fall. Rain squalls can occur in spring and summer, for these mountains seem to make their own weather.

With the winter season a backpacker here is likely to see a true "snowbird," the Carolina junco, which braves the cold weather in the region. A small gray bird with white breast, it is commonly observed in the higher elevations. Any large black birds spotted winging over the mountain summits are likely to be ravens, generally rare in the Southeast, but frequently seen in this region.

According to U.S. Forest Service figures the Shining Rock Wilderness in fiscal year 1978 had 308,000 visitor days, which makes it the most heavily visited wilderness in the Southeast and one of the most popular in the entire nationwide wilderness system. Most of those visitors have discovered what the wilderness brochure warns against: "Danger ahead . . . for those who may have a tendency to become addicted to quiet, peaceful beauty . . . ."

HOW TO VISIT SHINING ROCK WILDERNESS

This 13,600-acre wilderness is at once both remote and accessible, for it is located near the town of Brevard and the Blue Ridge Parkway, but its winding hiking trails lead to the rooftop of the Smokies at an elevation of over 6000 feet.

To enter the wilderness from the Blue Ridge Parkway, exit at milepost 420.2, which is Forest Service Road 816. This road leads 1.5 miles to a dead-end parking lot and the trailhead for the path to the Shining Rocks. Another entrance into the wilderness is off U.S. 276 as it crosses the East Fork of the Pigeon River on the eastern boundary. A third entrance is along N.C. Highway 215, the area's western boundary.

HIKING AND BACKPACKING: Backpacking into the high, crisp air is the main attraction of this wilderness, which is in dramatic contrast to the nearby Linville Gorge Wilderness, also located in the Pisgah National Forest. There are approximately 25 miles of trails within the wilderness, most of them fairly steep but short. It is possible to combine several trails for extended long-distance hiking.

One of the most popular trails is the Art Loeb Trail, a 6-miler that leads from the FS 816 parking lot to the Shining Rocks which named the wilderness, and then continues on to the summit of Cold Mountain. The Shining Rocks are approximately halfway up this trail, 3 miles from the parking lot. From the parking lot off U.S. 276, it is also possible to hike up to the Shining Rocks following the 4.5-mile Shining Creek Trail. The elevation change along this trail is over 2500 feet, much of it seemingly coming during the last steep climb up to the rocks.

All trails are well blazed, and intersections are signed. Although the trails are steep in places, hikers' efforts are rewarded by spectacular vistas from the mountain summits. Because of the moderately difficult hiking, day packers should allow ample time for their trips.

CAMPING: Camping is permitted throughout the wilderness, but backcountry-use permits are required. They may be obtained in advance from U.S. Forest Service offices in Asheville and Pisgah Forest. A number of primitive campsites are located along different trails and U.S. Forest Service rangers prefer that campers use these whenever possible. Fires may be built, but portable stoves are recommended to lessen the danger of wildfire. Water is available in numerous springs and creeks but should be purified before drinking.

Backpackers and campers should try to purchase a USGS topographic map of the area, the Shining Rock, N.C. quadrant.

Numerous other national forest campgrounds are located nearby along U.S. 276.

FISHING AND HUNTING: Hunting for deer, bear and wild boar is popular in the region during season. Most activity centers in the Sherwood Wildlife Management Area.

Trout fishing is especially popular in the area's rivers and small streams. The East and West Forks of the Pigeon River, Shining Creek, Yellowstone Branch and Greasy Cove Prong all support brook and rainbow trout.

Fishermen and hunters will need a state license, a special trout license and a game lands permit. Fishing on certain waters may be limited to three days per week only. For additional information concerning fishing and hunting regulations, contact the North Carolina Wildlife Resources Commission, 512 North Salisbury, Raleigh, NC 27611.

WILDLIFE OBSERVATION: Wildlife is fairly plentiful in the region, and careful campers might see bear, whitetail deer, squirrel and fox. Wild boar range throughout this portion of the state, and evidence of their presence will probably be seen in the wilderness, although hikers may not see the animals themselves.

CANOEING AND RAFTING: The waters within the Shining Rock Wilderness are not especially suited to rafting or canoeing, but other nearby rivers are. Portions of the French Broad, Tuckaseegee and Little Tennessee are extremely popular and challenging white-water runs. For additional information on paddling these rivers, contact the Nantahala Outdoor Center, Star Route, Box 68, Bryson City, NC 28713.

ADDITIONAL INFORMATION: For complete information on the Shining Rock Wilderness, contact the District Ranger, P.O. Box 8, Pisgah Forest, NC 28768.

JOYCE KILMER/SLICK-ROCK WILDERNESS
"A Memorial to Poet Joyce Kilmer"

Early in this century a young writer named Joyce Kilmer penned the immortal poem "Trees." Today, long after Kilmer's death in Europe during World War I, a living memorial to him in the North Carolina Mountains draws thousands of visitors each year. It is the 3800-acre Joyce Kilmer Memorial Forest, which the poet himself surely would have enjoyed seeing.

The forest contains more than a hundred species of trees, several of them over 300 years old. The largest measure 20 feet in diameter and spread their canopies higher than 100 feet above the ground. Yellow poplar, hemlock, beech, oak and sycamore all are found here. On the forest floor are the remains of once-great chestnut trees, killed during the blight introduced in 1925 from Asia in which all of this nation's chestnuts were destroyed.

Adjoining the Kilmer Memorial Forest is the Slickrock Wilderness, with nearly 12,000 additional acres of rugged, rolling Appalachian ridges. To the west are the Unicoi Mountains, to the south are the Snowbirds and northward is Great Smoky Mountains National Park, so the entire region is one of high summits, deep gorges and heavy forest.

Parts of this wilderness are virgin forest, and those areas that have been logged have grown back well. According to the U.S Forest Service, the Babcock Lumber Company began logging along Slickrock Creek in the northern part of the wilderness in 1915 and constructed a small railroad beside the stream to haul out the timber. In 1922 the company had to stop harvesting because Calderwood Dam on the Little Tennessee River flooded a large part of its railroad. The land was later purchased by the Forest Service. The Kilmer Memorial was established in 1936.

In addition to its trees, the forest contains a rich variety of shrubs, ferns, mosses and wildflowers. In spring and early summer, parts of the mountainsides turn pink with the blooms of mountain laurel, rhododendron and wild azalea.

Clear streams follow many of the valleys through the wilderness, and in most of them wild trout still thrive; several, such as Slickrock and Santeetlah, have gained national fame for their brook trout populations. Each stream is characterized by numerous small falls and deep pools. In some areas only fly fishing is permitted. Backpacking trails follow many of these streams, providing the opportunity for fine backcountry camping/fishing excursions. There are more than 60 total miles of trails in the wilderness, many connecting at various junctions for extended hiking or short loop possibilities. There are also several short day-use only trails in the memorial forest.

This is vertical country, with elevations ranging between 2000 and 5300 feet. Most hiking on the trails involves climbing, with some steep ascents, so hikers should be prepared for strenuous travel. Camping is permitted throughout the wilderness but not in the memorial forest.

The Nantahala National Forest is the former hunting ground of the Cherokees, who called it the "land of the noonday sun" since so many of the deep valleys received the full light of the sun only at midday. This area is also the beginning of the dreadful Trail of Tears, on which about 13,000 Cherokees were forced by General Winfield Scott to march from these mountains to a new reservation in Oklahoma in 1838.

Wild game still abounds in the region and includes black bear, deer, turkey and ruffed grouse. Wild boar are sometimes encountered by hikers, and a few are taken each year by hunters. Throughout the spring and summer numerous songbirds can be found in the memorial forest.

The area receives moderate visitation, most of it, of course, in the memorial forest which is a day-use only area. Even in summer, evening temperatures are cool, and in fall the mountainsides turn orange and red with the changing leaves. Snow can be expected in the winter months.

The Joyce Kilmer Memorial Forest has been preserved as a tribute to the author of the famous poem "Trees." There are over 100 species of trees in the Kilmer forest, some of them more than 300 years old.   Photo by U.S. Dept. of Agriculture

HOW TO VISIT JOYCE KILMER/ SLICKROCK WILDERNESS

The Joyce Kilmer/Slickrock Wilderness is located northwest of Robbinsville, North Carolina, in the Nantahala National Forest. It can be reached by taking U.S. Highway 19 south from Bryson City and turning northwest on U.S. 129 toward Robbinsville. Approximately eight miles beyond Robbinsville, turn west on N.C. Highway 1127 which leads to the Joyce Kilmer picnic area.

HIKING AND BACKPACKING: An extensive trail system has been designed in this wilderness area, crisscrossing the area from several directions. The Joyce Kilmer Memorial Forest has day-use trails only, the Slickrock Wilderness several overnight hiking possibilities. Many visitors backpack through the Joyce Kilmer Forest into the wilderness area where overnight camping is permitted. Three such routes are the Naked Ground, Haoe and Stratton Bald trails which climb 4.5, 5.5 and 8.5 miles respectively to the higher ridges. The Haoe and Stratton Bald trails follow the wilderness boundaries and eventually join the Naked Ground Trail, making several loop connections available.

Traveling south from the town of Tapoco on U.S. 129 and turning west on Forest Service Road 62 offers access to several other trails north of Joyce Kilmer Memorial Forest. The Hangover Lead Trail follows the wilderness boundary south to connect with the Haoe Trail near Saddle Tree Gap. The Hangover Lead Trail also can be hiked northward to Yellowhammer Gap where it connects with the Ike Branch Trail, a three-miler that leads back to Lake Calderwood in Tapoco. At Yellowhammer Gap several other trails can be picked up, including the Yellowhammer Gap/Nichols Cove Trail, which eventually meets the Slickrock Creek Trail.

Most of these backpacking trails are well marked and wind through beautiful scenery. The Unicoi Mountains are just to the west in Tennessee, with many of the ridges measuring between 4000 and 5000 feet.

CAMPING: Primitive-type camping is permitted in the wilderness, but no over night camping is allowed within the Joyce Kilmer Memorial Forest. Campfires made from dead-and-down wood are permitted in the wilderness, but backpacker stoves are recommended. Water is available from area streams but should be sterilized before drinking.

One national forest campground, Horse Cove, is located on a stream very near the entrance to the forest and offers the closest nonwilderness camping opportunities. Cheoah Point campground is another small Forest Service campground located nearby on Lake Santeetlah.

HUNTING AND FISHING: Hunting is permitted in the Nantahala and adjoining Cherokee national forests for bear, deer, grouse, turkey and squirrel in season. This is part of the Santeetlah Wildlife Management Area.

Fishing is quite good within the Slickrock Wilderness and forest, and Little Santeetlah Creek (the Naked Ground Trail follows this stream) is probably one of the most popular trout streams in the state. Wild brook trout are the most well-known species here. Other streams include Big Santeetlah, Slickrock, Bear, Barker and Rock creeks, all of which are relatively remote and provide fair to good fly fishing. These streams are normally open only three days per week and on major holidays during the trout fishing season, and require a special game lands permit in addition to a North Carolina fishing license. For a short portion of its length, Slickrock Creek forms the boundary between Tennessee and North Carolina; anglers should either purchase licenses for both states or remain on only one side of the water. Good bass and walleye fishing is also available in nearby Santeetlah, Calderwood and Fontana lakes.

For additional information, contact the North Carolina Wildlife Resources Commission, 512 North Salisbury, Raleigh, NC 27611; or the Tennessee Wildlife Resources Agency, P.O. Box 40747, Ellington Agricultural Center, Nashville, TN 37204.

WILDLIFE OBSERVATION: Backcountry campers might see bear, deer, turkey, squirrel and raccoon in the region. Several species of hawks are regularly observed soaring above the higher ridges, and ruffed grouse might be heard drumming in the deep forests. Backpackers might also encounter the area's two poisonous snakes, the timber rattler and copperhead, along some of the trails. The best spots for wildlife observation and photography are within Joyce Kilmer

A backpacker rests for a few minutes enjoying the tremendous scenery of Slickrock Wilderness.

Memorial Forest for squirrel, deer and songbirds; deeper in the Slickrock Wilderness bear might be found along some of the lesser-used trails and near the laurel thickets on the mountain slopes.

RAFTING AND CANOEING: Streams within the wilderness do not lend themselves to rafting or canoeing, but several other rivers nearby provide fine white-water trips. The Nantahala River flowing beside portions of U.S. 19 north of the U.S. 129 junction is rated as one of the top white-water streams in the Southeast, with nearly eight miles of continuous rapids. Parts of the Little Tennessee and the Tuckaseegee rivers also offer fine canoeing and rafting. Guided trips and canoe rentals are available from the Nantahala Outdoor Center, Star Route, Box 68, Bryson City, NC 28713.

ADDITIONAL INFORMATION: For additional information on the Joyce Kilmer/Slickrock Wilderness, contact the Superintendent, Nantahala National Forest, P.O. Box 2750, Asheville, NC 28802.

SOUTH CAROLINA

Visitors to the Palmetto State have discovered South Carolina offers more than cotton plantations and tobacco farms. The northwest corner of the state catches the last ridges of the Blue Ridge and borders on the famous Chattooga River. Along the southeastern coast in Francis Marion National Forest, backpackers will discover slow-moving inky waters, mossy cypress trees, old Indian mounds and Revolutionary War battle sites. In between these two regions, there are two divisions of the Sumter National Forest, near Greenwood and Union, as well as a number of challenging rivers to paddle. Sumter officials also administer regulations concerning the Chattooga.

Geographically Columbia, the capital, is near the center of the state, and major north-south and east-west expressways lead from here to the different recreation areas. Airline connections are good.

Wildlife is abundant in this varied terrain, with whitetail probably the most commonly seen animal. The state has one of the longest deer hunting seasons in America to help control expanding deer populations. Wild turkey are also plentiful, as are wintering waterfowl.

CONGAREE SWAMP NATIONAL MONUMENT
"Walking in a Forest of Giants"

Just 20 miles south of Columbia, the capital city of South Carolina, stands a tiny patch of 18th-century wilderness, virtually undiscovered until the 1950s and now recognized as one of the most unusual tracts in the entire National Park System. It is officially known as the Congaree Swamp National Monument, a 21,000-acre primeval forest of giant trees, many of which were already old when George Washington was President. In contrast to most of today's American forests which are second- and third-growth timber, a portion of the Congaree, known as the Beidler Tract, has never seen an ax.

As a result some of the trees here are enormous, towering over 150 feet into the air and having a circumference of over 20 feet. Park officials use binoculars to study the leaves. Of the 35 species of trees thus far identified in the Congaree, 24 have been designated as state or national champions — the largest on record.

One of the national record holders is the loblolly pine, which really does not even belong in the Congaree; it is not a swamp dweller, does not normally mix with hardwoods and rarely lives to be 200 years old. In the Congaree, however, the largest loblolly, measuring 15 feet, 10 inches in circumference, 150 feet in height and having a canopy spread of 87 feet, is estimated to be over 300 years old. Nearby are numerous others believed to have lived over 200 years. One loblolly stump was located that had 320 rings.

Other national record trees here include the bitternut hickory, swamp privet, possum haw, sweet gum and overcup oak. State record trees include red maple, sugar maple, persimmon, sycamore, numerous oaks and other hardwoods. Botanists and park officials say there may be even more record trees or possibly larger ones than those already recorded in the swamp; they just have not found them.

It is a healthy forest, for most trees are big and few are blighted. However, there are few new trees sprouting. Because the older specimens blot out the sunlight with their enormous canopies, new generations of trees cannot gain a foothold.

The Congaree is not a true swamp, but instead must be classified as an alluvial floodplain, flooded eight to ten times annually by the Congaree River. On the south side of the river steep bluffs rising over 200 feet in places force the floodwaters over the low, relatively flat north bank. This area is approximately ten miles long and extends some three miles inland from the river to another line of low bluffs. The Congaree Swamp is contained between these two dominant geologic features.

Throughout this 30-square-mile area, there are dozens of tiny pothole ponds and narrow winding ditches. The water flowing in these waterways changes direction according to the level of the Congaree. One major stream, Cedar Creek, remains actively flowing throughout the year.

There is little underbrush in the swamp, a condition caused by the covering canopy of the trees and the frequent flooding. Thick vines and creepers dangle from many of the trees, and some approximate the size of trees themselves, with diameters of nearly a foot. Dense canebrakes dominate the riverbank of the Congaree and in places along Cedar Creek, but generally the forest floor provides easy travel.

Upon entering the swamp, there is no immediate indication of the presence of big timber. The narrow logging road twists and dips deeper and deeper into the woods. Suddenly the first loblollies come into view, giant forest sentinels guarding each side of the road to form a fence over 100 feet tall. The national record loblolly is off to one side, nearly hidden among the hardwoods.

One must walk to see the huge cypress and tupelo gum trees. Growing in tangled profusion along one of the swamp's many ditches, the cypress knees alone may be over six feet tall. During the dry season walking is easy, but when the Congaree floods only the tips of these cypress knees may be above water. For this reason, there is little small game in the Congaree. Deer are here, with some wild turkey, but the primary residents are birds. The air is alive with songs from dozens of different species, and some believe the ivory-billed woodpecker may still survive here.

There is evidence of early humans in the region, for sand bars along the Congaree frequently yield bits of pottery and flint. Early settlers grew rice and raised cattle in the Congaree valley, and to protect their livestock from the floods, constructed high earthen mounds. Several mounds have been found in the swamp, one measuring nearly 100 feet long, 50 feet wide and 6 feet high.

Some portions of the Congaree have been logged, for the land has been in the private ownership of one family since about 1890. Between 1890 and 1905 Francis Beidler, a Chicago timber executive, purchased over 100,000 acres of South Carolina swampland, including the Congaree hardwoods. His principal interest at that time was cypress, and the hard, slow-growing trees were especially abundant along the Congaree, Wateree and Santee rivers. The logging industry had spread throughout the South by this time, and during the next quarter century most of the southern forests were cut. All

A park official measures one of the huge cypress trees in the Congaree Swamp. Numerous state and national record trees have been discovered in this new park, and others are probably waiting to be found.

species of trees went before the ax, but the durable cypress, which extended from the Atlantic to the Midwest, were nearly wiped out. The trees were girdled, not only to kill them, but also to lighten them enough with the resulting loss of sap so they could be floated downriver to the nearest sawmill.

Logging on the Beidler property ended about 1910, and the land, handed down to each succeeding generation of the family, remained essentially undisturbed for nearly 50 years. Much of the total Beidler property now lies beneath the waters of the Santee-Cooper lakes complex. Another portion has been designated as the Francis Beidler Forest, part of the Four Holes Swamp National Audubon Sanctuary northwest of Charleston which contains the largest stand of virgin tupelo in the world.

On October 18, 1976, Congress established the 21,000-acre Congaree Swamp National Monument to preserve the remaining 11,000-acre tract of virgin hardwoods and portions of the surrounding forest. There are no visitor facilities within the Congaree; park headquarters is located in Columbia.

HOW TO VISIT CONGAREE SWAMP NATIONAL MONUMENT

Visitation into the Congaree Swamp National Monument is extremely limited and generally is open to small groups and clubs rather than individuals. This will change as facilities are constructed and the number of park personnel is increased.

A park management plan presently under study calls for limited development of the area with utmost care taken to protect the fragile qualities of the swamp. A Visitor Center along the swamp's northern boundary would include an information desk and interpretive facilities, and possibly would mark the starting point for a system of self-guiding trails. At present the only access roads into the Congaree are logging roads that frequently require the use of four-wheel drive and are not suitable for today's low-clearance automobiles.

Construction of a one-way loop road for vehicles is under consideration, but this road would be only slightly improved for smoothness and probably would not be paved.

The Congaree is located approximately 20 miles southeast of Columbia, near S.C. Highway 48 and the town of Gadsden.

FISHING AND HUNTING: Hunting is not permitted in the swamp except to members of the Cedar Creek Hunt Club, who have been leasing the hunting rights to the area for many years. The club's hunting rights will continue for several years.

Fishing is allowed in the Congaree River for largemouth bass, bream and catfish. Some of the swamp's interior ponds and sloughs may be opened to public fishing in the future as a management plan develops.

WILDLIFE OBSERVATION: A number of endangered species might be seen in the Congaree, including Swainson's warbler, the Mississippi kite and the swallow-tailed kite. Southern bald eagles and red-cockaded woodpeckers are also seen occasionally. Beside the river visitors might expect to see great blue herons, common egrets and, in winter, various species of ducks. In the swamp's interior bobwhite quail, American woodcock and wild turkey are year-round residents. In all, over 125 species have been recorded here.

Mammals present include deer, raccoon, mink and squirrel.

CAMPING: At present no overnight camping is permitted within the park boundaries. In the future a primitive campground may be opened for limited overnight camping.

Campsites are available at Poinsett State Park near Wedgefield and Wateree, as well as at Santee State Park near Santee. For information write Poinsett State Park, Wedgefield, SC 29168; and Santee State Park, Rt. 1, Box 255-A, Santee, SC 29142.

HIKING: Hiking is the best way to see the Congaree, but because of the lack of trails, visitors must either follow the logging roads of strike out through the swamp itself to see the big trees. The park management plan calls for construction of several trails and regularly scheduled naturalist-led walks.

ADDITIONAL INFORMATION: For additional information, contact the Superintendent, Congaree Swamp National Monument, P.O. Box 11938, Columbia, SC 29211. If your club or group plans a visit to the Congaree, please notify the superintendent well ahead of time.

TENNESSEE

The very crest of the Appalachians forms Tennessee's eastern boundary, producing some extremely wild and rugged terrain. The Appalachian Trail follows this crest for miles, and backpackers can look over huge vistas of rolling forests and steep gorges. Numerous clear cold rivers and streams cascade down out of these mountains, providing exciting rafting and canoeing experiences as well as good trout fishing.

Eastern Tennessee also includes part of Great Smoky Mountains National Park, with its accompanying 6500-foot peaks, winding trails and trout streams. The park is one of the most heavily visited national parks in the nation throughout the spring, summer and fall.

Wildlife in this portion of the state includes black bear, whitetail deer, wild boar, ruffed grouse and some wild turkey. Quiet backpackers and paddlers are likely to see one or more of these species during a weekend trip. It is easy to see why Davy Crockett liked the state.

Gateways to the mountains are Chattanooga, Knoxville and the tri-cities area of Bristol, Kingsport and Johnson City. From each of these cities it is but a short drive into the mountains of the Cherokee National Forest and the Great Smoky Mountains National park is very near Knoxville. Air travel into these cities is available.

Fall is a spectacular time to pack or paddle here, with crisp breezes and changing leaves. Summer evenings will be cool, but daylight hours can get warm.

SAVAGE GULF AND GREAT STONE DOOR
"The Crow's-Foot Canyon of the Cumberlands"

One of the South's least known wilderness tracts is the 13,000-acre Savage Gulf State Natural Area and the adjacent Great Stone Door State Environmental Educational Area, located approximately 50 miles northwest of Chattanooga near the small town of Palmer. It is a rugged chunk of canyonland that takes a visitor by surprise, for the land suddenly drops away to depths of 800 feet or more in three long, intersecting canyons.

Here the major gorges of the Collins River, Big Creek and Savage Creek cut into the Cumberland Plateau like a giant crow's foot, forming miles of sheer rock cliffs. Above is a pine and hardwood forest that appears relatively unchanged from centuries past. At the western edge of this wild countryside is one of the few natural passages down into the canyon itself, a crack in the sandstone cliffs known as the Great Stone Door, which leads to a large spring the Cherokees once used.

The history of Savage Gulf extends far beyond the Indian nations who once called the Cumberland Plateau home. These rocks and cliffs are as much as 300 million years old, deposited as the floor of a shallow ocean that once washed over this land. As the seas receded, water runoff gradually formed what is known today as the Collins River and its tributaries. These streams quickly began carving their signatures through the soft sedimentary rock, a process still going on.

The Great Stone Door gateway into the gorge was also formed at this time, as the earth trembled and shuddered in growing pains. A huge spring began bubbling from the floor of the gorge below the notch in the cliffs.

This spring was utilized by the Indians until they were driven out by the encroaching white man's civilization. The spring was then "rediscovered" by Mrs. Beersheba Cain in 1833, who, believing the water held medicinal qualities, returned often to drink and bathe there. Within ten years of Mrs. Cain's discovery, a small community sprang up on the mountain ridge several miles away. It was named Beersheba Springs and soon became a resort town on the road between Chattanooga and McMinnville.

Resort activities ended with the onset of the War Between the States, and the town never really regained its footing afterward. The property went through a succession of owners until finally being acquired by the state and established as a natural/scientific area in 1973. Development now is restricted to footpaths, footbridges and overlooks.

This is fine hiking and backpacking country, for several trails wind along the very edges of the different canyons, and two lead down the steep cliffs to the streams below. The trails, maintained by the Tennessee Trails Association, are well marked and easy to follow. Except for the descents into the gorges, the trails are not steep and wind through a forest of

A backpacker crosses one of the area's small streams on a narrow wooden bridge. Trails here lead to the edge of Savage Gulf, down into the canyons and through the Great Stone Door, a natural notch in the canyon walls.

oak, maple, dogwood, poplar, hickory and holly. The forest floor is a mixture of flowers, mosses and ferns.

On some of the trails, a casual hiker may notice that in places it seems as if small pieces of coal are present. Much of this region is underlaid with coal seams, formed when advancing oceans washed across the then-existing forests.

In order to protect the region as much as possible from human impact, a permit system is in effect for all backpackers, and camping is allowed only at specific sites. These are all primitive campgrounds, usually with nothing more than cleared underbrush and pit toilets. At the halfway point of the North Plateau Trail loop, campers are allowed to use the old Hobbs hunting cabin, which has six wire bunks, a picnic table and an outdoor fireplace. It is the only sign of civilization in the area.

HOW TO VISIT SAVAGE GULF

Savage Gulf State Natural Area is located on the edge of the Cumberland Plateau, near the town of Palmer, Tennessee, approximately 50 miles northwest of Chattanooga. Follow Tenn. Highway 108 north through Palmer about one mile, and turn right on a paved county road where a sign points to Savage Gulf. Follow this road five miles, and turn left at another Savage Gulf directional sign onto a gravel road. This road leads to ranger headquarters about 0.5 mile away.

It is also possible to enter the Savage Gulf from Beersheba Springs. Driving on Tenn. 56 north from Altamont, turn right in Beersheba Springs on the paved road just beyond Beersheba Springs park and follow it to the ranger station. There are no signs.

HIKING AND BACKPACKING: Several trails are open to day and overnight hikers here, leading along the canyon rim and into the gorge itself. All are extremely well marked and easy to follow, and only those descending into the gulf have steep climbing. Trailheads are located near the Palmer and Laurel Falls ranger stations.

The shortest day hike is the four-mile Savage Falls Trail, a short loop leading to a scenic waterfall on Savage Creek at the very head of the gorge. Beginning from the Palmer entrance, this trail winds easily through a mixed pine and hardwood forest and is not strenuous. From the falls overlook, a hiker can envision what the terrain ahead will look like.

This trail intersects the North Plateau Trail, an 18-mile loop along the edge of the canyon. Just before reaching this intersection, hikers will come to an overlook of the gorge itself, but this is just a preview of the countryside. The forests are thick, the canyon walls sheer rock clifffs. This overlook shows the gorge at its narrowest point.

The North Plateau Trail eventually intersects with the Stone Door Connector Trail, a rugged ten-miler leading down into the gulf and following the floor of the canyon to Great Stone Door campsite near the Laurel Falls Ranger Station.

From this ranger station, two more day hiking trails are available, the seven-mile Laurel Falls Trail and the eight-mile Big Creek Gulf Trail. The Laurel Falls loop follows the rim of the canyon, while the Big Creek Gulf Trail descends to the floor of the gorge, meets the Stone Door Connector Trail, then ascends to rejoin the Laurel Falls Trail near Stone Door campsite.

The Savage Gulf canyons are formed by the Collins River and two major tributaries, Savage Creek and Big Creek. In places the canyons are 800 feet deep, with sheer rock walls.

WILD PLACES OF THE SOUTH

CAMPING: All but one of the campsites in this wilderness are primitive ones that have been cleared out of the woods. Camping in any other areas is prohibited. Water is available at nearby ranger stations and from streams and springs. Camping permits are required, and in extremely dry weather no campfires may be permitted. All trash must be packed out.

Campsites are available at the beginning of the Savage Falls Trail, along the back loop of the North Plateau Trail, at the Hobbs Cabin, below Laurel Falls at the Stone Door, and at the edge of the gorge on the Laurel Falls Trail.

The only non-primitive camping area is the Hobbs Cabin, located at the junction of the North Plateau and Stone Door Connector Trail. A former hunting camp, it includes six wire bunks, a picnic table and a small stone grill. There is flat tenting space adjacent to the cabin for use when the building is full. All sites are available on a first-come, first-served basis.

HUNTING AND FISHING: No hunting is allowed in the canyons or on the Great Stone Door Environmental Education Area property, but state-managed two- and three-day deer hunts are conducted on various weekends during the season. Ruffed grouse and squirrel are also hunted in season on the north plateau. During the entire deer season the Stone Door Connector Trail is closed to backpackers.

Fishing in the region is good for trout and largemouth bass, primarily in areas outside canyons. The Collins River and its tributaries are good trout waters above the gorge. Nearby reservoirs Nickajack, Woods and Tims Ford have thriving populations of largemouth, smallmouth and striped bass.

Additional information concerning hunting and fishing regulations is available from the Tennessee Wildlife Resources Agency, P.O. Box 40747, Ellington Agricultural Center, Nashville, TN 37204.

WILDLIFE OBSERVATION: The varied terrain and elevation changes produce a habitat supporting a wide range of wildlife in Savage Gulf. Whitetail deer might be seen on the north plateau, as well as squirrel and rabbit. Bobcat and fox inhabit the region but will seldom be observed by the casual hikers. Two species of poisonous snakes, the copperhead and the rattlesnake, are also found in the area. Deep in the forests a backpacker might hear the distinctive drumming of a ruffed grouse or see one of the popular game birds near a woodland trail.

RAFTING AND CANOEING: Float-tripping down the canyons is not permitted.

A nearby canoe outfitter, Scott Pilkington of Dunlap, does offer canoe rental for trips down the scenic Sequatchie River. Over 100 miles of this river may be floated. For additional information, write Sequatchie River Canoe Rentals, Box 211, Dunlap, TN 37327.

ADDITIONAL INFORMATION: Additional information and maps of the region are available from the Superintendent, Savage Gulf State Natural Area, Route 1, Box 127-H, Palmer, TN 37365; and from the Tennessee Trails Association, Inc., P.O. Box 4913, Chattanooga, TN 37405.

THE NOLICHUCKY RIVER

"The Cherokee's River of Destruction"

The water has always been there. First as part of an ocean, sweeping far inland across the North American continent when the earth was young. Then as huge isolated lakes when the sea began to recede again; and finally as rivers when the land became restless, buckled and faulted, giving birth to the Appalachians.

The Appalachians, stretching from Quebec to Georgia, are America's oldest mountains, dating back in places hundreds of millions of years. But some of the rivers are even older. The Nolichucky of western North Carolina and eastern Tennessee is one such river, and its cold water still churns and rumbles today through a deep forested gorge just as it has for untold centuries.

The Nolichucky begins in the North Carolina mountains northeast of Asheville near the small town of Poplar. Here the Cane and Toe rivers join, and many local residents refer to the Nolichucky simply as the Big Toe. The river flows northward, then west, then south, getting stopped in Tennessee at Davy Crockett and Douglas lakes. At Douglas Lake near Newport, the French Broad meets the Nolichucky to become the mighty Tennessee River, which flows 650 miles to meet the Ohio which in turns flows into the Mississippi. Thus rainfall and melted snow from western North Carolina eventually winds up in New Orleans.

The Nolichucky is a wild river for only part of its length, primarily along a nine-mile section in the Pisgah and Cherokee national forests where it flows through a steep canyon known as the Nolichucky Gorge. Here the average gradient is about 36 feet per mile—enough to produce nearly continuous rapids. In one particularly rugged mile the river drops 66 feet, twisting and turning through a maze of rocks and narrow channels with rapids rating to a very challenging Class 4.

The river rapids can be described mainly as ledges and drops, with big roller-coaster waves and few quiet pools. Most of the rapids require precise maneuvering, but the river can be run with an open canoe. The life expectancy of a raft on the Nolichucky is short because of all the rocks.

The one thing that has kept the Nolichucky from being named a national wild and scenic river is the Clinchfield Railroad which runs along the river right through the gorge. Dating to the early 1900s, the railroad still has heavy use transporting coal across the South.

Above the railroad and the river, the mountain slopes rise in a series of steep ridges, all heavily timbered in a wide variety of hardwoods and evergreens. Strangely, however, the timber is absent from many of the mountain summits. There are over a hundred of these "balds" as they are known between Georgia and Virginia, varying in size from less than an acre to over 100 acres, and geologists and botanists have been trying to fathom their existence for years.

This region has more than 130 species of trees—more than all of Europe—and many of them, like poplar and hemlock, grow to huge dimensions. But the balds are completely treeless and contain only few shrubs and grasses. There is no evidence of past fires, and the soil is rich and deep.

The Cherokees called the balds *Udawagunta* and believed they were inhabited by a giant hornet that flew down from the treeless summits to capture young children. The monster was finally tracked to a cliffside cave high on one of the cloud-shrouded ridges, and there the Cherokees, with help from a lightning bolt from the Great Spirit, were finally able to slay the hornet. The Great Spirit then ruled that forevermore the mountain summits would remain treeless so the Cherokees could keep watch for other hornet monsters.

The word *Nolichucky* is also from the Cherokee tongue, and roughly translated means "river of destruction" or "river of death." The origin has been lost to history, but a study of the river's rapids will leave little doubt of the Nolichucky's awesome power.

Rapids begin soon after the put-in point and continue steadily through the gorge. The most notorious rapid is probably

Quarter Mile, with a Class 3 entrance that quickly turns into a long, wild cascade of Class 4 (Class 5 at higher water levels) ledges, boulders and deep holes. There are few quiet eddies, and rescue is difficult. From Quarter Mile, the Nolichucky immediately rolls into Roostertail, Loner, Roly-Poly, Roller Coaster, and No-Name rapids, all Class 3 white water.

As the Nolichucky flows out of the gorge, the water finally calms. Most float trips end at the railroad trestle at Unaka Springs just south of Erwin. While the river is paddled safely by numerous rafters, canoeists and kayakers each year, it would be wise to travel this waterway first with an experienced Nolichucky outfitter. Like all rivers, its mood changes dramatically with different water levels.

Everybody paddles on the Nolichucky, for once the rapids begin at the head of the Nolichucky Gorge, they continue for nine miles, with many rating up to Class 4.

Outfitters provide lunches on rafting trips, and here a party of paddlers stops on a sand bar for a noon swim and some sandwiches before continuing down the river.

HOW TO VISIT THE NOLICHUCKY RIVER

Because the Nolichucky flows through a deep gorge cutting through national forest lands, there are few places for windshield views of the river. The Appalachian Trail follows the high ridges above the Nolichucky along Unaka Mountain and actually crosses the river just south of Erwin, Tennessee, providing the best views of the gorge.

It is possible to see some of the river by following Tenn. Highway 30 out of Erwin into the Cherokee National Forest to Indian Grave Gap. This marks the boundary line between Tennessee and North Carolina, and the road becomes Forest Service Road 230, leading near the small town of Poplar, North Carolina, put-in point for rafting and canoeing trips.

Even though Erwin is actually the takeout point along the river, it should also be considered the gateway to the Nolichucky, for the town offers accommodations, campgrounds and restaurants, and two outfitting organizations are located here. Erwin is approximately 18 miles south of Johnson City on U.S. Highway 19W/23 and 55 miles north of Asheville on U.S. 23.

RAFTING AND CANOEING: The Nolichucky is a favorite of white-water enthusiasts throughout the South and East, for once the rapids begin, they seldom slow down for the next nine miles through the Nolichucky Gorge. Little rafting is done on the Nolichucky once the river leaves the canyon.

Because the river quickly becomes unfloatable at higher water levels, first-time visitors would do well to float or paddle the river with an experienced outfitter. The commercial rafting season normally begins as early as April and continues through October, depending on the weather. Wet suits are recommended for spring trips, but are not needed in the fall.

Rafting trips last from five to seven hours, depending on the flow of the water and the number of stops made for swimming, picture taking and bailing. Outfitters like to begin around 9:00 a.m. and provide a sandwich lunch on the riverbank. Paddles and life preservers are also provided. Raft trips cost approximately $30.00 per person, and some minimum age limits may be in effect.

Rafters can expect to get wet and should dress accordingly. Swim suits worn under light trousers, long-sleeved shirts and tennis shoes are recommended.

Outfitters offering commercial rafting trips on the Nolichucky include Nolichucky Expeditions, Inc., Box 484, Erwin, TN 37660; Black Canyon Expeditions, Erwin, TN 37660; Wildwater Ltd., Long Creek, SC 29658 (winter address: 400 West Road, Portsmouth, VA 23707); and New River Outfitters, Inc., Rt. 1, Box 123, Green Mountain, NC 28740 (winter address: 206 Blowing Rock Road, Boone, NC 28607).

HIKING AND BACKPACKING: The best backpacking in the region is along the Appalachian Trail, which winds the full length of the Cherokee National Forest after leaving Great Smoky Mountains National Park at Davenport Gap. A full description of the trail is covered in the book *Guide to the Appalachian Trail in Tennessee and North Carolina, Cherokee, Pisgah, and Great Smokies.* This is one of several trail guides available from the Appalachian Trail Conference, Inc., P.O. Box 236, Harpers Ferry, WV 25425.

Trail access points in the region include U.S. 421, north of Mountain City, Tennessee; Tenn. 91, south of Shady Valley; the Lake Watauga Dam and overlook area; U.S. 19E near Laurel Falls; the Nolichucky River south of Erwin; U.S. 19W at Spivy Gap; U.S. 23 at Sams Gap; N.C. 208 (Tenn. 70) at

The Nolichucky Gorge cuts deeply through the mountains of western North Carolina and eastern Tennessee; only a railroad, built early in this century, keeps the Nolichucky from becoming a national wild and scenic river.

Allen Gap; U.S. 25/70 at Hot Springs, North Carolina; and I-40 at the Big Pigeon River. Portions of the trails are extremely steep, and backpackers should plan their schedules carefully. Some trail shelters are located in the national forests.

CAMPING: Camping is permitted throughout both the Cherokee and Pisgah national forests. The nearest national forest campground to the Nolichucky is Rock Creek, located several miles from Erwin. Another convenient campground is Limestone Cove near the town of Unicoi just north of Erwin. South of Erwin are Horse Creek and Old Forge campgrounds, also maintained by the U.S. Forest Service.

WILDLIFE OBSERVATION: The Nolichucky Gorge is one of the South's largest bear habitat areas outside Great Smoky Mountains National Park, but river runners seldom see bear or any other wildlife because they are too busy negotiating rapids. There is a high deer population here, and early morning rafters or canoeists might see one at the water's edge.

The best opportunities for wildlife observation and photography are on the hiking trails above the river. These woods also contain ruffed grouse, wild turkey, fox, squirrel and raccoon.

HUNTING AND FISHING: Hunting and fishing are popular in both the Cherokee and Pisgah national forests.

Fishermen can challenge brown and rainbow trout, catfish and bass in the region's many streams and lakes. The Nolichucky itself is popular among anglers in the calmer water just above Erwin. Other favorite waters include the French Broad, Little Pigeon and Little Tennessee rivers, as well as Watauga, Holston and Boone reservoirs.

Area hunters may go after deer, turkey, grouse, squirrel, fox and raccoon in season. Some wild boar hunting is also practiced in the area.

For additional rules and regulations, contact the Tennessee Wildlife Resources Agency, P.O. Box 40747, Ellington Agricultural Center, Nashville, TN 37204.

ADDITIONAL INFORMATION: Additional information on the Nolichucky River and Gorge is available from any of the commercial river outfitters listed, as well as from the U.S. Forest Service, Forest Supervisor, P.O. Box 400, Cleveland, TN 37311.

TEXAS

Within its huge borders, the Lone Star State contains two of the most awesome wilderness areas of the United States. These are Guadalupe Mountains National Park near the New Mexico border, and the canyons of the Rio Grande River of Big Bend National Park along the Mexican border.

A visitor to Texas notices immediately the tremendous distances that must be traveled between different areas. It usually takes a couple of days of driving just to cross the state, even though its roadways are among the best in the nation! Despite this handicap, outfitters and guide shops have sprung up throughout the state and are busy introducing Texans and others to the wilderness experience. There are many miles of floatable water, ranging from placid to boiling. Backpackers are challenging the dry deserts of Big Bend or the Guadalupe Mountains. Nearly all land in Texas is privately owned, however, so hiking opportunities are limited; some national forest trails exist in eastern Texas.

Texans are fond of saying that if you do not like the present weather situation, just wait a couple of minutes and it will change. Often this seems to be the case. Storms blow across the Panhandle and upper plains with alarming speed, bringing ice and even snow, while the southern border counties will be experiencing short-sleeve temperatures.

BIG BEND NATIONAL PARK
"Where the Rainbows Wait for the Rain"

"You go south from Fort Davis until you come to the place where the rainbows wait for the rain, and the big river is kept in a stone box, and the water runs uphill, and the mountains float in the air, except at night when they go away to play with other mountains."

This colorful description, reportedly penned years ago by a Spanish vaquero, paints an accurate picture of one of America's most stunning wilderness areas, Big Bend National Park in far south Texas. Here, in this vast untrammeled terrain, the Chihuahuan Desert rises suddenly into the Chisos Mountains nearly 8000 feet high; the mighty Rio Grande cuts its way through awesome canyons; and the ghosts of past Comanche and Apache war parties still ride the whirling winds.

It is big country, tough and lonesome and often unforgiving. The saying here is that a car is shiny but a burro is sure. A car breakdown may mean a wait of hours or a walk of miles for help.

Big Bend became a national park in 1944 and embraces 708,221 acres. Some think the land was too tough even for Texas to handle, so the state simply declared it a national park and gave it away. Big Bend's history is a fiery, violent one and dates back over 100 million years. Water then covered the region as part of what is now the Gulf of Mexico. Gradually the ocean receded as volcanic thunder uplifted the land, forming mesas, mountains and jagged ridges. Beginning first as ocean runoff, the Rio Grande easily cut through the soft sediments until it had actually boxed itself into several deep, winding canyons. Time and erosion are still completing the work.

There are three major river canyons inside the park and several others outside the boundaries that are among Big Bend's primary attractions. Santa Elena, the most well known of these gorges, is approximately nine miles in length. Canyon walls rise steeply to 1500 feet straight from the river's edge and may be only 50 feet apart from top to bottom. This is the vaquero's "stone box."

Santa Elena is not the longest of the Rio Grande canyons, nor is it the roughest in terms of rapids. The other park canyons, Mariscal and Boquillas, are longer but not quite as awesome. Outside the park, the Lower Canyons of the Rio Grande stretch for over 100 miles through truly wild, desolate country.

The park was established to protect this unique desert/ mountain/river ecosystem, and even today development has been kept to a minimum. You can best explore Big Bend by horseback, riding to the South Rim and overlooking the edge of the Chisos Mountains and the desert plain below; by foot, backpacking along miles of lonesome faded trails to the ruins of forgotten ranches; and by water, paddling by raft or canoe through the winding canyons.

Although much of Big Bend is desert-type terrain, rains come up suddenly, occasionally with disastrous flooding. After

The canyons of Big Bend are awesome in their size and their abruptness. Here a raft prepares to enter Santa Elena Canyon, the park's most famous gorge, where the river flows through a "stone box" for ten miles. Lower Rio Grande canyons outside park boundaries are even larger.

any rain shower the desert changes color dramatically as dozens of plants and shrubs burst into bloom. Truly, the "rainbow waits for the rain." Often, too, the Chisos Mountains appear and disappear in the early morning haze, giving ghostly images of stark peaks and rugged canyons. It is a timeless, mesmerizing land, both geographically and historically. Dinosaurs once roamed here, and their bones have been unearthed along canyon walls. Indian artifacts and wall paintings decorate many a cave. And a ghost town nearby stands as mute testimony to an enterprise that tried and failed.

HOW TO VISIT BIG BEND NATIONAL PARK

The main entrance into Big Bend is along U.S. Highway 385 south of the small town of Marathon. This is the same route followed by raiding Comanche war parties over a century ago, and it leads directly into the Chisos or "ghost" Mountains and park headquarters. These volcanic peaks stand like a rocky fortress above the rolling desert sands and harbor a completely different community of plants and wildlife.

BACKPACKING AND HIKING: Visitors may first want to try the Lost Mine Trail along the entrance into the Chisos Basin to see if hiking is really the way they want to visit Big Bend. This short trail climbs to the summit of Lost Mine Peak, at an elevation of over 7500 feet. The trail is paved, easy to follow and leads through a changing community of plants as the elevation rises.

There are a number of other backpacking trails in the Deadhorse Mountains, the Sierra Quemada (Burnt Range) and other portions of the park. Trails range up to about 25 miles in length; most are extremely rugged and often difficult to follow. Many cannot even be found without knowing how to read a topographic map. Backcountry permits are required, and park rangers should be contacted prior to any trip for current information about trail conditions. Snakebite kits should be carried, even in winter.

The Deadhorse Mountains are the most remote part of the park, and no reliable water supply is available. Hikers are advised to carry at least one gallon of water per person per day in this region. The Sierra Quemada extends from the South Rim

This is basically desert country, with yucca and cactus often dominating the landscape. There are numerous backpacking trails in the park, but water is usually scarce.

to the Rio Grande, and water is available. Wildlife is abundant. Other hiking trails lead to Apache Canyon, Burro Mesa and Mariscal Mountain. Write for the park information sheet, "Hiking Off the Beaten Path," at the park supervisor's address given below.

CANOEING AND RAFTING: Guided raft trips are available down Santa Elena Canyon, the Lower Canyons of the Rio Grande (actually downstream from Big Bend National Park), and Colorado Canyon, which lies west of the park.

The Santa Elena trip lasts two days, and trips begin at the tiny settlement of Lajitas, just outside the park's western boundary. Overnight camp is made on the riverbank at the head of the canyon. The only rapids are those of the "rockslide" located approximately one mile inside the nine-mile canyon.

The Lower Canyons trip lasts six days and covers 90 miles of extremely rugged, isolated canyon country. Four major rapids are encountered, and natural hot springs abound. It has been termed by some as one of the premier river runs in North America.

Colorado Canyon is a six-hour trip through a lava flow with

numerous rapids. This trip is occasionally combined with the Santa Elena trip as a four-day, 50-miler.

The outfitter for all of these trips is Far Flung Adventures, headquartered in the ghost town of Terlingua. On all trips safety is a major concern, and life preservers are provided. Rafters must bring only their own sleeping bags and eating utensils which will be lashed to the rafts in waterproof containers. Meals are furnished and include steaks, enchiladas and shrimp creole — all prepared over charcoal fire.

Many adventurers paddle the various Rio Grande canyons, but this is not country for the inexperienced; it is a harsh, unforgiving land where the nearest help will be many miles distant. And once into any of the river canyons, the paddler is committed to completion of the trip, with or without a boat.

For additional rafting information contact Far Flung Adventures, P.O. Box 31, Terlingua, TX, 79852; or Whitewater Experience, 3835 Farnham, Houston, TX 77098.

FISHING AND HUNTING: Hunting is not permitted within the boundaries of Big Bend National Park. Some hunting for antelope and mule deer is occasionally provided by landowners in the vicinity.

The only fishing permitted inside the park is in the Rio Grande, where there is no closed season and no license is required. Catfish and perch are the most frequently sought-after species, with some catfish reaching weights of over 100 pounds.

Outside the park Texas fishing licenses must be purchased.

For additional information, contact the Texas Parks & Wildlife Dept., 4200 Smith School Road, Austin, TX 78744.

WILDLIFE OBSERVATION: The Big Bend country teems with an amazing variety of animal life, but many of the species are seldom seen by visitors unless they penetrate the backcountry. There are panthers here, along with whitetail and mule deer, pronghorn antelope, javelina, fox and squirrel. Deer may be seen along some of the park roads at dawn and again at sunset; antelope are occasionally spotted in some of the broad basins; panthers are almost never sighted. Over 200 species of birds have been identified in the region.

The flora is equally diversified, ranging from desert cactus to mountainous ponderosa pine. Some of the more unusual plants of Big Bend include Mexican drooping juniper, a tree found only in the Chisos Mountains that always appears wilted;

One of the ways to explore this wilderness is by horseback. Day trips and overnighters are possible. The massive rock in the background here is Casa Grande near the park entrance.

skunkbush sumac, a plant closely related to poison ivy but not poisonous and once used by Indians to make dyes, baskets and even a refreshing drink; and lechuguilla, a cactus-looking plant that actually belongs to the same family as the daffodil.

CAMPING: Backcountry camping is permitted anywhere within Big Bend free of charge. A backcountry-use permit, available from park headquarters, is required.

Established campgrounds operated by the National Park Service are open in the Chisos Basin, Rio Grande Village near Boquillas Canyon, Santa Elena Canyon and Castolon. Recreational vehicle sites are available at Panther Junction (park headquarters) and Rio Grande Village. Campgrounds throughout the park do not all provide the same facilities. Sites at Santa Elena Canyon and Castolon, for instance, are limited to basic sanitary facilities, a limited number of grills and tables and water that may or may not be potable.

No reservations are needed for park camping. No open fires are permitted anywhere in the park. Food can be purchased at Castolon, Chisos Basin, Panther Junction and Rio Grande Village. In addition, a modern restaurant and comfortable cabins are available at Chisos Basin.

ADDITIONAL INFORMATION: For more information, write the Superintendent, Big Bend National Park, TX 79834.

GUADALUPE MOUNTAINS NATIONAL PARK
"To the Top of Texas"

Guadalupe Mountains ranks as one of the nation's most unusual national parks, for not only does it embrace the world's largest exposed fossil reef dating back 280 million years, but also because its 76,293 acres have remained essentially free of any development. It is a park for those who enjoy traveling on foot through rugged country where water is seldom available, living out of their packs in a rough and often harsh environment.

The rewards of such travel in the Guadalupes are many, however. The park is a meeting ground for a rare mixture of desert and mountain plant and animal communities, where elk and jackrabbit, cactus and fir tree, share the same living space. The mountain escarpment rises steeply off the dry desert floor — it can be seen for more than 100 miles — forming one of the most delicate ecological balances to be found anywhere in the world. Elevations vary from 3650 feet to over 8700 feet and include the highest mountain in Texas, 8749-foor Guadalupe Peak.

The amazing mountain range begins in far west Texas and extends 40 miles into New Mexico through Carlsbad Caverns. Then it actually goes underground for another 300 miles, swinging in a great loop near Hobbs, New Mexico, and back into Texas as far south as Alpine. The range surfaces there as the Glass Mountains, then continues underground again, only to surface once more as the Apache Mountains east of Van Horn.

Actually, these mountains are known to geologists as the Capitan barrier reef, formed between 225 and 280 million years ago when an inland sea covered several thousand square

144

miles of west Texas and eastern New Mexico. The mountains are primarily limestone, and in many places ancient fossils are exposed on the surface or in the canyon walls.

The Guadalupe escarpment ends abruptly at El Capitan, a massive stone fortress with a 2000-foot sheer rock face. From El Capitan the mountains extend northward in a slight V formation; this feature is one of the characteristics that makes the park so exciting to backpackers. Inside this V, an area known as the Bowl, is a lost world where the desert is suddenly left behind. In its place is a cool, refreshing mountain forest of aspen, fir and ponderosa pine where wild turkey, elk and even black bear may be found.

Water is the common bond that ties this intricate balance of life together in the Guadalupes, for it is scarce everywhere in the park, even in the high country. Only in some of the canyons and at several springs is water available throughout the year. McKittrick Canyon is one such canyon, and wild trout swim in the icy waters of one of its streams. Here, too, the canyon walls are etched with the history of ages past, for the actual core of the ancient reef is visible.

Man made his way into these mountains about 12,000 years ago, living in cliffside caves, hunting the abundant wild game and harvesting various types of cactus. Spanish explorers probably trekked across parts of the Guadalupes, but for hundreds of years the land belonged to the people who later came to be known as the Apaches.

Numerous army survey expeditions between 1840 and 1856 skirted the edge of the escarpment, and in 1858 the Butterfield stage line established a station at Pine Springs, the location today of the park's major campground. The station was open for only a year — ruins are still visible near the campground — but the route west had been established and in ensuing years thousands of white settlers pushed through the region.

Skirmishes and raids by the Apaches became a way of life in the Guadalupes, just as in the Chisos Mountains to the south in present-day Big Bend National Park. Eventually the Indian threat was overcome and the land opened for cattle ranching. Remains of several early ranches are still visible in the park.

Two modern-day ranchers, J.C. Hunter, Jr., and Wallace E. Pratt, came to own most of what is now the national park. Both men recognized the spectacular beauty of the mountains and its unique ecology, and both helped restore various species of wildlife to the area. Hunter stocked the trout in McKittrick

Canyon and aided in bringing elk back into the highlands. Pratt donated 5632 acres of his holdings to the National Park Service between 1958 and 1961, and five years later Guadalupe Mountains National Park was authorized by Congress. The Hunter property was acquired soon after, and in 1971 the park was formally opened.

Visitors today will find things little changed from the days before this area was a national park. There are no facilities for motoring tourists such as motels, cabins or restaurants, and there are no scenic drives. The one paved road in the region, U.S. Highway 62/180, does provide excellent vistas of the escarpment with Guadalupe Peak, El Capitan and other high summits. A ranger station/information office known as Frijole Station is located along this highway and is the only source of water for the area. A small campground will accommodate tents and self-contained recreational vehicles.

Steep trails lace out from the campground and various other spots in the park leading up the canyons to the summit of Guadalupe Peak and into the Bowl. Winter will bring heavy snow to the highlands, and rapidly falling temperatures to the lower regions. Summer temperatures are extremely hot.

The massive peak of El Capitan, with its 2000-foot sheer rock face, marks the southern boundary of the Guadalupe escarpment in the park. It is part of an ancient reef created over 250 million years ago when an inland sea covered this part of Texas and New Mexico.

Mule deer are common throughout the park. Other game includes elk, fox, porcupine and rabbit. Unconfirmed sightings of mountain lion and bighorn sheep have been reported.

HOW TO VISIT GUADALUPE MOUNTAINS NATIONAL PARK

Guadalupe Mountains National Park, the "top of Texas," is located in the far western part of the state along the New Mexico border. It is approximately 110 miles east of El Paso and 55 miles south of Carlsbad, New Mexico, along U.S. 62/180. Park headquarters is located in Carlsbad, but a visitor information office is located on U.S. 62/180. The park can be reached by following Texas Highway 54 north from Van Horn; or take U.S. 285 north from Pecos, then Tex. 652 west from Orla and head south on U.S. 62/180.

The park receives its heaviest visitation in the spring, especially during college holidays, but fall is possibly the most pleasant time to visit. In October average temperatures range between 46 and 68 degrees, with little rainfall.

HIKING AND BACKPACKING: Guadalupe Mountains National Park is a hiking and backpacking park due to its lack of development. The only hard-topped road in the park is U.S.

147

62/180, which skirts only the southern boundary, but there are 63 miles of hiking trails. These trails normally follow game paths or old wagon routes and have not been highly developed. Most are rocky and in places quite steep.

The major consideration for all backpackers here is water. There are few regular sources for water anywhere in the park except at the Frijole ranger station. Hiking cross country off the established trails is discouraged, and no open fires are permitted. Backcountry-use permits are required and may be obtained in advance from park headquarters in Carlsbad or from the ranger stations in Dog Canyon and McKittrick Canyon. Backcountry camping is limited to designated campsites.

Several trails begin at Pine Spring campground, including the popular but steep climb to the summit of Guadalupe Peak. This eight-mile round trip to the highest point in Texas can be made in a single day. Another day hike leads approximately six miles from the campground to Devil's Hallway, a very narrow but scenic portion of Pine Canyon. Overnight trips can also begin at the campground by following the Pine Top Trail or the Bear Canyon Trail, both of which are less than three miles long and lead into the higher elevations known as the Bowl. Each trail is characterized by steep switchbacks and an ascent of more than 2000 feet.

Once into the high country, backpackers can follow several additional routes including Bush Mountain, Blue Ridge Mountain, Juniper, Tejas or Hunter Peak trails, which form various loop possibilities. The hiking in the Bowl is through heavy forest in contrast to the barren slopes, and the increased elevations offer spectacular views of the Chihuahuan Desert and salt flats far below. There are four designated campsites in this trail system.

The second major trailhead is McKittrick Canyon, where the McKittrick Trail leads four miles along the canyon floor then climbs steeply to Turtle Rock and on to the junction of the Lost Peak Trail, a distance of about five additional miles. It is then possible to follow the Lost Peak Trail across the ridges to either the Mountain or Tejas trails and eventually descend to the Pine Spring campground. There are two backcountry campsites along the way.

McKittrick Canyon also provides a fine day hike trail, approximately six miles round trip, leading from the parking lot to the McKittrick Canyon ranger station. The trail passes through a variety of desert and mountain flora, while the surrounding cliffs provide a unique study in geology dating back millions of years.

A third trailhead is Dog Canyon campground, where backpackers can climb into the high country via both the Marcus and Lost Peak trails, then continue along the Lost Peak or Tejas trails to connect with the remainder of the park's trail system. Several of these trails are difficult to follow and are marked with rock cairns.

CAMPING: The park's one established campground is Pine Spring, located just off U.S. 62/180. It is a primitive campground with approximately 20 drive-in sites. There is no water or electricity. Camping here is free, and no backcountry-use permits are required. Charcoal grills, picnic tables and chemical toilets are provided. Camping is also permitted at Dog Canyon in the northern part of the park. Development plans call for 15 sites, but do not include facilities for RV users. Water is scarce and may not be available.

There are a number of designated campsites along the park's different hiking trails which campers are required to use. Water is scarce throughout Guadalupe Mountains National Park, so backpackers must carry water with them.

WILD PLACES OF THE SOUTH

HUNTING AND FISHING: No hunting is permitted in Guadalupe Mountains National Park. There is good hunting for both mule deer and antelope on the Texas ranches south of the park, but seasons are normally quite short. There is also good mule deer hunting in the Lincoln National Forest of New Mexico adjoining portions of the national park.

Although there are trout in one stream within the park, no fishing is permitted. The nearest fishing is in Red Bluff Lake, about 60 miles east of the park, or in some of the national forest streams.

For additional information on hunting or fishing, contact the Texas Parks and Wildlife Department, 4200 Smith School Road, Austin, TX 78744; or the New Mexico Department of Game and Fish, State Capitol, Santa Fe, NM 87503.

WILDLIFE OBSERVATION: Numerous species of wildlife can be seen in the park, even by those who do not hike into the high remote regions. Mule deer can usually be found between Pine Spring campground and the Frijole ranger station along U.S. 62/180 early and late each day. A small herd of elk is also present in the park and is frequently seen near Manzanita and Smith Springs just beyond the Frijole ranger station.

In the Bowl hikers might see wild turkey, raccoon, porcupine, fox and possibly bear. More than 200 species of birds and 70 species of reptiles and amphibians have also been identified in the park.

ADDITIONAL INFORMATION: For additional information, contact the Superintendent, Guadalupe Mountains National Park, 3225 National Parks Highway, Carlsbad, NM 88220.

Several publications may be helpful in planning a trip to the park. These include "Trails of the Guadalupes," ($1.25) and "Guadalupe Mountains National Park" ($1.75). Both are available from park headquarters.

VIRGINIA

The theme "Virginia is for lovers" certainly can be applied to those who love backcountry hiking or quiet country canoeing. The Mount Rogers National Recreation Area, located in the southwestern portion of Virginia, is a popular setting for back-packing, and includes two peaks over 5000 feet. The Appa-lachian Trail passes through this area. And practically any-where a lover of history might turn, there are historic battle-fields of the Civil War. Shenandoah National Park is perhaps the most famous of these sites, and is extremely popular among campers as well as history enthusiasts.

An entirely different type of terrain exists in the south-eastern part of the state, the Dismal Swamp. Today the swamp is but a small fraction of its former size, but still retains its mystery and charm.

It is easy to travel throughout Virginia, even though these three major outdoor recreation areas are spread far apart. Suf-folk, Galax and Charlottesville are the major gateway cities, but expressways crisscrossing the state make accessibility quick and easy from all cities.

The higher altitudes of the Jefferson National Forest mean cooler spring and summer temperatures, and these are ideal times to be afield. Winter will bring snow, occasionally even in-to Dismal Swamp.

DISMAL SWAMP
"Nature's Marvelous Mistake"

Centuries ago when the land was still young, Mother Nature just may have had an accident that caused the creation of one of the South's most unusual wild areas, Great Dismal Swamp. It is truly a paradox in the botanical and geological world, for Dismal Swamp is not a low-lying basin like most swamps, but rather a hillside. Instead of being open and wet, Dismal Swamp is practically solid forest, and its wettest season is also its driest. Lake Drummond, 3000 acres in the swamp's interior, is not the lowest point in Dismal Swamp, but one of its highest.

Although man has "challenged, cursed, coveted and celebrated" Dismal Swamp, today's visitor will find it an intriguing place that is not dismal at all. There are seven distinct ecosystems here, ranging from upland forests and pine barrens to cane thickets, cypress lowlands and evergreen bogs. A fraction of its former size, it contains 210,000 acres of which 76,000 acres is administered as Dismal Swamp National Wildlife Refuge. The swamp straddles the Virginia/North Carolina border, south of Portsmouth.

No one really knows how Dismal Swamp originated. Peat began accumulating in the area between 6000 and 9000 years ago, and there is evidence this region was once under the ocean. Some believe beavers caused the swamp, cutting trees to dam the rivers draining the area and creating a bog. A swamp-type ecosystem took over, and Great Dismal eventually was formed. Geologists believe the lake may have been created when a long-burning peat fire cleared the area; other guesses include the falling of a meteorite. The easiest explanation to digest for the swamp's origin is that Mother Nature just made a mistake one day during her busy schedule of aligning things.

The center of the Dismal Swamp is Lake Drummond, a shallow 3000-acre lake colored dark by the bark of different trees. It is sweet, rich water, and some say Commodore Perry filled his barrels with Dismal Swamp water before departing on his epic sailing expedition to Japan. The lake's primary source of new water is rainfall.

Lake Drummond was named for William Drummond, who is thought to have discovered the lake around 1655. He later served as the first governor of North Carolina between 1663 and 1667. The actual origin of the name Dismal Swamp is uncertain, although it is recorded by 1727 in official government writings. William Byrd, who helped survey the region in 1728, disliked the swamp and called it a dismal place. George Washington did not think of Dismal Swamp in those terms. After his first visit in 1763, he suggested draining it with a north-south canal in order to open up more farmland and to connect Chesapeake Bay with Albemarle Sound as a new shipping route.

Washington began his canal that year, eventually completing a five-mile stretch from the swamp's western edge to Lake Drummond. Today his channel is known as the Washington Ditch, and the dike built by his labor is one of the swamp's major access roads. His agricultural attempts failed, however, so he turned his attention to harvesting the region's rich timber resources (but this did not succeed either).

Patrick Henry, who also owned Dismal Swamp property, liked Washington's idea of an interstate canal and helped push through state authorization for construction of such a waterway. Work began in 1793 and the canal was opened in 1805. Today, after widening and deepening, that original canal is still in use — the Dismal Swamp Canal that follows U.S. Highway 17 north along the eastern edge of the swamp.

Practically the entire Dismal Swamp has been harvested by different timber companies, for the area contained the nation's largest stand of Atlantic white cedar as well as substantial growths of tupelo gum and even pine. Union Camp Corporation established one of the principal logging operations in the swamp and continued cutting until the mid-1940s. In 1973 Union Camp formally deeded its land holdings in Dismal Swamp to the Nature Conservancy, which conveyed the land to the U.S. Department of the Interior for management as part of Dismal Swamp National Wildlife Refuge.

153

From atop one of the fire towers, Dismal Swamp seems to stretch unbroken for miles. The swamp is but a fraction of its former size, yet still covers more than 200,000 acres, much of it now a national wildlife refuge.

The refuge is unusual in that its function is more for management of the swamp's unique ecosystems rather than for its wildlife. There is wildlife here — more than twice as many mammals are reported in Dismal Swamp as in the Everglades — but it is seldom seen. Black bear, whitetail deer, otter, mink, bobcat, rabbit, raccoon and squirrel all call the swamp home. About 75 species of birds are known to nest here, and several hundred have been identified as migratory visitors. One entomologist identified 73 separate species of butterflies in just one corner of the swamp, and a springtime visitor will see many of these during a swamp tour. Copperhead, cottonmouth and rattlesnake are also found here.

There are fish in the lake and canals, but not many. Catfish is the most abundant, with various sunfish, crappie and pickerel also present. The darkness of the water prevents photosynthesis from occurring, keeping the lake biologically poor. As a result, there are few wading birds seen here.

Like all swamps, the area is rich in legend and lore, many of the stories dating from before the Civil War when the swamp was often a hideout for runaway slaves. Longfellow wrote about Dismal Swamp in his poetry, and Harriet Beecher Stowe wrote of it in novels.

One of the most well-known legends is that of the deer tree. A forest witch tricked hunting dogs by changing herself into a deer and leading them on a merry chase through the woods. Upon reaching Lake Drummond once, she waded out into the water, then changed herself into a cypress tree to keep from being caught. Alas, she is never able to turn back into a deer or a witch. The old-timers in the swamp can point out the very tree she changed herself into.

Besides looking for the deer tree, swamp visitors on Lake Drummond on some foggy summer night may see a white canoe across the water carrying an Indian maiden and her brave. He will be paddling, she guiding the way with a lamp of fireflies.

With its aura of mystery, its remote beauty and its history, such a story of Dismal Swamp is easy to believe.

HOW TO VISIT DISMAL SWAMP

Access to Great Dismal Swamp is easy. Travel south on Va. Highway 642 (Whitemarsh Road) from the city of Suffolk. Jericho and Washington Ditch roads, both located off this

Canoeists paddle the quiet waters of Lake Drummond at dawn. The lake is actually one of the higher points of Dismal Swamp and covers about 3,000 acres. Average depth is about six feet.

road, mark with yellow gates the refuge boundaries. Auto traffic is not permitted beyond these gates, but roadside parking is allowed, and visitors may travel on foot or by bicycle.

Refuge headquarters is located at 680-B Carolina Road (U.S. 13 and Va. 32), approximately 1.5 miles south of downtown Suffolk.

Boat access is via the Lake Drummond Feeder Ditch from the U.S. Army Corps of Engineers dock and ramp along U.S. 17, approximately ten miles north of South Mills, North Carolina.

HIKING AND BACKPACKING: Hiking must be limited to day walks only along the various spoil bank roads. The refuge is open year-round from sunrise to sunset, and no permits for entry are required, although refuge officials prefer that visitors check in at headquarters first. Hikers should plan to carry bug repellent and wear long trousers and long-sleeved shirts. Maps available from the refuge office show the best hiking areas.

The main pathways in the swamp are spoil bank roads along the various drainage ditches and canals. Jericho Ditch and Washington Ditch are the primary canal roads, but visitors can also travel on Corapeake, East, Railroad and Interior Ditch roads, each of which leads to Lake Drummond.

Along Washington Ditch it is approximately five miles to the shore of Lake Drummond. Jericho Ditch leads about eight miles to the lake. The roads will be muddy after heavy rains, but both provide easy access routes during dry weather.

Free public tours are offered by refuge staff personnel between April and November. These tours are limited to 20 persons, and advance reservations are required. Travel is by minibus or auto, and visitors must bring their own lunches and drinking water. Tour schedules are announced several months in advance. For additional information, contact the Dismal Swamp National Wildlife Refuge, P.O. Box 349, Suffolk, VA 23434.

CANOEING AND RAFTING: One of the best ways to visit Dismal Swamp is by canoe or small motorboat. Water access to the swamp is along U.S. 17, approximately ten miles north of South Mills, North Carolina, along the eastern edge of the swamp. A U.S. Corps of Engineers dock and ramp (signs mark the location) is available for use free of charge.

Canoes may be rented at this ramp from Alvah Duke's Dismal Swamp Boat Tours restaurant. Fiberglass canoes rent for $2.00 per hour or $10.00 per day (anything over five hours is charged as full-day rent). Overnight rates are $15.00, and extra day rentals are $7.00 per day. Paddles are included. The address is Alvah Duke's Dismal Swamp Boat Tours, 4107 George Washington Highway, Chesapeake, VA 23322.

From the landing on U.S. 17, it is possible to paddle up the Feeder Ditch three miles to the Lake Drummond spillway. There, boats can be loaded on a motorized tram (1000-pound limit) for the short portage back into the Feeder Ditch. Lake Drummond is 0.5 mile further down the ditch. The lake's shoreline is marked with craggy cypress and the water is pure and dark. Average depth is about six feet.

Canoes are also available for rent at Chesapeake Campground, located on U.S. 17 several miles north of the Corps boat landing. Rates are $2.00 per hour, $10.00 per day or $48.00 per week per canoe. For further information, contact Chesapeake Campground, 693 South George Washington Highway, Chesapeake, VA 23323.

From the landing on U.S. 17, it is also possible to view portions of Dismal Swamp by paddling or motoring along Dismal Swamp Canal, a waterway that parallels U.S. 17 and the edge of the swamp. This canal leads from Norfolk/Portsmouth to the Pasquotank River near Elizabeth City. Locks are located at Deep Creek and South Mills, the northern and southern boundaries of the swamp.

FISHING AND HUNTING: Hunting is extremely limited in Great Dismal Swamp. Various clubs have leased hunting rights on the nonrefuge portions of the swamp, and the only hunting permitted within the refuge itself is a controlled whitetail deer hunt each fall. For additional information, contact the Dismal Swamp Refuge office.

Fishing is only fair in the swamp, a condition caused primarily by the water's high tannic acid content. The best fishing occurs during the spring months when anglers may catch crappie, bream and catfish. Fishing is permitted only in Lake Drummond and in the Feeder Ditch between sunrise and sunset. A Virginia state fishing license is required. For information, contact the Commission of Game and Inland Fisheries, 4010 W. Broad St., Box 11104, Richmond, VA 23230.

Butterflies are common in Dismal Swamp in the spring; over 70 different species were once recorded by an entomologist in just one corner of the swamp.

WILDLIFE OBSERVATION: The best opportunities for wildlife observation and photography occur along the spoil bank roads. Game often travels along these roadways when moving from one area to another. Whitetail deer are the most commonly seen mammals, while snakes and turtles can usually be spotted along the ditches or sunning on logs. Bear and turkey are both present in Dismal Swamp but seldom seen by the casual visitor. These animals remain deep in the swamp's hidden pockets and are rarely seen even by refuge personnel.

More than 75 different bird species have been identified in Dismal Swamp, some of the most common being bobolinks, grackles, prothonotary warblers and vireos. There are no eagles here and few long-legged waders. Some loons have been seen on Lake Drummond, and various owls, hawks and hummingbirds have been observed along the ditch roads. Some of the most productive birding areas are located where two or more ditch roads intersect, such as at the Jericho, Hudnell and Lynn crossroads. When completed in mid-1980, an interpretive boardwalk near Jericho Ditch will offer fine birding opportunities, since it will wind through several separate plant communities of the swamp.

CAMPING: No overnight camping is permitted within Dismal Swamp National Wildlife Refuge.

The only camping within the swamp itself is located at the Feeder Ditch spillway and includes picnic tables, water and several tent sites. Access is by boat only, and camping is free. No reservations are required. Plan to cook with portable stoves or charcoal, since no wood is available. For information, contact the U.S. Army Corps of Engineers, 803 Front St., Norfolk, VA 23510.

Private Chesapeake Campground offers easy access to Dismal Swamp. Sites for tents as well as for recreational vehicles (including water, electricity and sewer hookups) are available. Rates range from about $5.00 per night for tents to $6.76 for full RV hookups. The campground offers tennis, horseback trail rides, hay wagon rides, roller skating, swimming pool, game room, canoe rental, laundry facilities and a small grocery store. Contact Chesapeake Campground, 693 South George Washington Hwy., Chesapeake, VA 23323.

WILD PLACES OF THE SOUTH

ADDITIONAL INFORMATION: For additional information on Dismal Swamp, contact the Dismal Swamp National Wildlife Refuge, P.O. Box 349, Suffolk, VA 23434.

WEST VIRGINIA

It is practically impossible to think of West Virginia without thinking of the Monongahela National Forest. This 833,729-acre sea of spruce and hemlock blankets the slopes and ridges of both the Appalachians and Alleghenies and has become the focal point for most West Virginia backcountry excursions. Amazingly, this huge forest is just 60 years old. In 1920 trees were scarce and there was virtually no wildlife, the result of uncontrolled timber harvests and massive wildfires.

Bogs, or glades in which a strange mixture of shrubs and trees are found, are interesting features of the Monongahela. The bogs are a holdover from the last Ice Age. There are also hundreds of miles of hiking trails, some of the East's most challenging rivers and great varieties of wildlife.

West Virginia transportation centers around Charleston, the capital, from which it is a two-hour trip by car to the southern edge of the Monongahela. Once in the forest, numerous U.S. and state roads provide breath-taking drives to the northern boundaries. Campgrounds are abundant.

Outdoor recreation is recognized as a major part of the state's tourism industry, and the Department of Commerce in Charleston keeps updated lists of various outfitters providing rafting, hiking and cross-country skiing excursions.

THE GAULEY RIVER
"Floating the Rolling Thunder"

Throughout the South and East, white-water canoeists, kayakers and rafters all have their favorite rivers. West Virginia claims many of these favorites, but one river often stands out above the rest. That river is the Gauley, which for 95 miles twists through the Mountaineer State between Jerryville and Swiss.

There are actually several sections to the Gauley, divided by various access points such as bridges or dams. The most popular and most awesome white-water runs are the 16-mile stretch from the Summersville Dam to Peters Creek and the 8-mile section between Peters Creek and the town of Swiss. Many like to make this combined 24-mile trip in two days, camping along the way. This portion of the Gauley flows through a remote, steep-walled canyon much of the way and contains about 100 rapids, most with colorful names like Lost Paddle, Five Boat Hole, Rattlesnake and Gateway to Heaven. At various water levels several of these rapids rate up to Class 6, which puts them in the same tough league with some of the Grand Canyon's Colorado River rapids.

The Gauley was reportedly first rafted in 1961 and not paddled until seven years later. Even then it took a contingent of some of the world's best white-water river runners to successfully navigate the boat-breaking falls and waves. Many of the rapids are extremely complex, requiring expert boat control and split-second maneuvering. This is a river for experts only.

The best way to see the Gauley is by rafting with one of several commercial outfitters. These trips are usually conducted in the fall months, generally after October 1, when

Summersville Lake is being drawn down and the river's water level is highest. Both one- and two-day trips are available. Several outfitters require that riders have previous rafting experience on other West Virginia wild waters such as the New or Cheat rivers before attempting the Gauley.

Paddlers should not try this river except in the company of others who have previously made the trip. The rapids rate as Class 4 practically at the put-in point and do not get much easier. Once in the canyon it is a one-way trip, too, broken boat/bones or not.

Because most Gauley runs are scheduled in the fall months when both air and water temperatures are colder, wet suits are recommended. Anyone on the river is going to get wet. Outfitters also supply life jackets and safety helmets, which are worn throughout the trip.

Here is a brief look at three of the Gauley River rapids encountered along the way.

The first rapid, easily visible from the parking lot below the Summersville Dam, is known as Initiation, and it is a fitting introduction to the river. Rated as Class 4, several outfitters, after running just this one rapid, pull back out of the water to make sure all their passengers still want to continue downriver!

Water splashes on board as a paddler strokes hard to keep from being swamped. Wet suits, life jackets and protective helmets are standard equipment on a Gauley River float trip.

WILD PLACES OF THE SOUTH

Pillow Rock is a 50-yard section of river several miles downstream where the water drops about 25 feet, churning up against massive chunks of sandstone and sweeping treacherously over others. It is Class 5.

At Iron Ring the river bends to the right, then drops down a six-foot slide to crash into a massive boulder. A Class 6 rapid, it usually spits out paddlers and boats in separate pieces. The name comes from a large iron ring set in the stone many years ago when loggers tried to dynamite some of the rocks away to allow logs to float freely down the river. The river's roar here is deafening.

The countryside that cradles the river is quiet and beautiful. Signs of civilization are scarce, and although a railroad track parallels the water for part of the distance, it is seldom used and not always visible. The fall brings changing colors and air that is crisp and fresh.

A driftwood beach fire is welcome during a lunch break on the Gauley. Anyone running the Gauley is going to get wet, and the lunch stop provides a chance to warm up again before hitting the next stretch of rapids.

HOW TO VISIT THE GAULEY RIVER

Because of its relative inaccessibility, there is little of the Gauley to see except from the seat of a boat or raft. The Summersville Dam parking lot, located near the town of Summersville (signs point to the dam), offers some indication of what lies downriver, but other vantage points are extremely difficult to locate.

CANOEING AND RAFTING: These are the best ways to see the Gauley, and guided raft trips are offered by numerous outfitters. A list of white-water guides is available from the Office of Economic Development, Travel Division, Capitol Building, Charleston, WV 25305.

All paddles, safety helmets and life preservers are furnished. On overnight trips outfitters provide all necessary food and equipment except sleeping bags and personal clothing. Rafts can carry up to eight persons, at least one and often two of whom will be qualified guides. If you are afraid of water or are a poor swimmer, this trip is not recommended.

FISHING AND HUNTING: The Gauley provides some trout fishing, although its inaccessibility limits the number of anglers who try their luck. Fine fishing is enjoyed in the lake and also right below the dam.

Hunting is permitted in the region and is popular in the nearby Monongahela National Forest for whitetail deer, wild turkey and black bear.

Hunting and fishing regulations are available from the Department of Natural Resources, 1800 Washington Street East, Charleston, WV 25305.

WILDLIFE OBSERVATION: Gauley River runners seldom have time to look for wildlife, but the river does pass through a region where several species of wildlife are abundant. Deer, black bear, wild turkey, fox, raccoon and squirrel are all present.

HIKING AND BACKPACKING: The nearby Monongahela National Forest contains dozens of miles of hiking trails and is far better suited to foot travel than the Gauley River gorge is. Information on hiking trails is available from the Supervisor,

WILD PLACES OF THE SOUTH

Monongahela National Forest, Box 1548, Elkins, WV 26241.

CAMPING: Camping is permitted along the Gauley River if one can find a level area. Other campgrounds are located nearby in the Monongahela National Forest and range from primitive sites to established campgrounds. A free brochure, "Camping West Virginia," is available from the Office of Economic Development, Travel Division (address above).

ADDITIONAL INFORMATION: Additional information on rafting or paddling the Gauley River is available from the excellent book *Wild Water West Virginia,* written by Bob Burrell and Paul Davidson. It is available for $6.00 from McClain Printing Co., Parsons, WV 26287.

Waves roll and paddlers stroke as their raft bucks through some of the most turbulent white water in the East.

THE OTTER CREEK WILDERNESS

*"Goodbye to Civilization
for a Day or Week"*

One of the first impressions a backpacker usually has of West Virginia's 20,000-acre Otter Creek Wilderness is that it seems much larger than it is, for the area is essentially roadless and embraces nearly the entire watershed of two streams, Otter Creek and Shavers Lick Run. Additionally, the area is bounded on the east and west by lofty mountain ridges that add to the sense of isolation. The area has been logged, first between 1890 and 1914, and again between 1958 and 1972. Still it has retained its wild flavor, for the second-growth spruce has recovered extremely well. The wilderness also has a mixture of hardwoods, as well as a small stand of virgin hemlock growing high on the ridge of Shavers Mountain. The understory is a dense jungle of rhododendron and mountain laurel, so most hikers elect to remain on the well-marked trails.

Like the Cranberry Back Country, the Otter Creek Wilderness includes several bogs, or glades, with their unusual vegetation more suitable to regions much further north. Such glades are usually the end result of past glacial activity and have remained soft, marshy and poorly drained. Trails lead beside each of these relatively small areas.

The many streams lacing through the wilderness present a tapestry of sparkling pools and low waterfalls, especially along Otter Creek itself. It is good habitat for a small population of brook trout, and fishing is permitted during the season for these square-tailed fighters. Only artificial flies and streamers are allowed, and anglers must release each fish they catch.

167

A backpacker fills his canteen from a cascading stream. This is a popular backpacking area in West Virginia, with numerous trails and outstanding scenery. The area was once logged but with proper management has almost completely grown back.

Camping opportunities are outstanding in this wilderness, for the Forest Service maintains two trail shelters, each located at strategic points on the area's two main trails. One appears approximately halfway along the Otter Creek Trail at its junction with the Moore Run Trail; the other is located on Shavers Mountain Trail not far from the stand of virgin hemlock. Each shelter will accommodate six campers, and the ground surrounding the three-sided huts is flat enough for additional tents.

Some of the earliest settlers in this region included a group of families from Switzerland who decided these heavily forested slopes were as inviting as their own European Alps and tried farming in the region around 1879. They named their settlement Alpina, which has since been changed to Alpena and is located just south of the wilderness boundary.

HOW TO VISIT THE OTTER CREEK WILDERNESS

The 20,000-acre Otter Creek Wilderness, established by congressional law in 1975 along with several other wilderness areas, is located in the northern portion of the Monongahela National Forest, approximately ten miles east of Elkins on U.S. Highway 33. This is some of the Mountaineer State's most scenic terrain, for a dozen miles further east stand the massive Seneca Rocks; to the south is Spruce Knob, highest point in West Virginia; and to the north is Dolly Sods, the spruce and lichen wilderness.

The area receives more than 55 inches of precipitation annually, often much of it at once. Foot-deep snows are not unknown, nor are 3-inch floods. Frost has been recorded in each month of the year.

Backpackers will occasionally see deer in the Otter Creek Wilderness, especially if they keep watch for them very early and late each day. Wildlife is making a comeback throughout the Monongahela National Forest; hunting is permitted in season for deer, turkey and bear.

HIKING AND BACKPACKING: The Otter Creek Wilderness contains nearly 50 miles of hiking trails, well maintained and marked by paint-slashed trees. The trails intersect throughout the wilderness so short one-day excursions or extended long-distance explorations are possible.

The two major trails in the wilderness are the Otter Creek Trail, 11 miles from north to south; and the Shavers Mountain Trail, 10.5 miles, also from north to south. The Otter Creek Trail largely follows an old railroad bed, so hiking is not difficult except at three creek crossings during periods of high water. This trail receives the heaviest use in the area, but other trails branching off from it are usually less crowded. The Shavers Mountain Trail follows the ridge of Shavers Mountain, which forms the wilderness boundary. The elevation here is about 3500 feet. The trail includes a number of steep ascents and passes a stand of virgin hemlocks, forest giants that have escaped both the ax and disease.

It is possible to hike from the Otter Creek Trail to the Shavers Mountain Trail along several branch trails, the longest of which is about five miles in length. These shorter paths offer a wide variety of terrain attractions, including glades, mountain vistas and clear-flowing streams.

CAMPING: Camping is permitted anywhere in the wilderness, but the Forest Service provides and encourages the use of two three-sided Adirondack-type shelters located on the Otter Creek and Shavers Mountain trails. These shelters, similar to those found on the Appalachian Trail, each accommodate six persons and are available on a first-come, first-served basis.

Camping permits are required of anyone entering the Otter Creek Wilderness and may be obtained in person or by writing or calling the U.S. Forest Service ranger offices in Richwood, Bartow, Petersburg, White Sulphur Springs, Marlinton, Parsons or Elkins.

Topo maps will be helpful in various wilderness activities. These quadrangles (all West Virginia) cover the entire area: Parson, Bowden, Harman and Mozark Mountain. Be sure to check out actual trail locations with U.S. Forest Service personnel.

HUNTING AND FISHING: Hunting is permitted in season for turkey, deer, grouse and various species of small game.

Trout fishing is permitted in Otter Creek but is restricted to

Many of the trails in the wilderness have unusual attractions, including boggy glades, mountain vistas and clear-flowing streams. Short day hikes are possible, as well as extended backpacking trips, on the nearly 50 miles of trails.

fly-fishing tackle only. All fish caught must be released immediately. The prevalent species is brook trout.

For additional information on fishing and hunting regulations, contact West Virginia Department of Natural Resources, 1800 Washington Street East, Charleston, WV 25305.

WILDLIFE OBSERVATION: This is one of several black bear sanctuaries in the state, and backpackers may catch sight of one of the bruins on some of the less traveled trails. Deer and turkey are also possible subjects for the camera, as are rabbits, the snowshoe hare and numerous species of birds. Hawks and occasionally golden eagles might be spotted following warm air thermals southward along the mountain ridges in the fall.

ADDITIONAL INFORMATION: Additional information on the Otter Creek Wilderness, including a descriptive brochure, is available from the Supervisor, Monongahela National Forest, Box 1548, Elkins, WV 26241; or from the District Ranger, U.S. Forest Service, Parsons, WV 26287.

THE CRANBERRY BACK COUNTRY
"Hiking the Boggy Highlands"

One of the easiest places to step from civilization to wilderness is the 53,000-acre Cranberry Back Country of West Virginia's huge Monongahela National Forest. Once completely cut over by early timber companies, this region has been closed to vehicular traffic since 1945 and allowed to redevelop into one of the most attractive areas in the state. Some 36,000 acres of the Cranberry Back Country are under study for inclusion in the Wilderness Preservation System.

Although much of this wilderness is typically West Virginia rugged with deep, steep-sided gorges and heavily forested mountain ridges, the most unusual area is known as Cranberry Glades, boggy wetlands just south of the boundary. In West Virginia there are several of these muskeg bogs known as *glades,* characterized by dense shrub thickets, wet moss-covered hummocks, and heavy spruce and hemlock forests. Normally such botanical mixtures are found only in the tundra regions much further north.

Cranberry Glades is the state's largest highland bog and covers approximately 400 acres. Botanists believe the unusual plant communities present may have been caused by the southward push of the glaciers 10,000 years ago. When the glaciers melted, they left behind what the ice had carried down —the ancestral seeds of the plants now growing here.

Two wild orchids bloom in the area, attracting numerous visitors during the summer months. In late June the pink snake-mouth orchid peaks, followed in July by the grass-pink orchid, a taller and brighter plant with flowers ranging from pink to dark red.

A visitor to the Cranberry Back Country today will find it hard to believe this forest is second-growth timber. The area was logged extensively by the Cherry River Boom and Lumber Company between 1920 and 1926, and later burned severely by lightning-caused wildfires. In 1934 the U.S. government purchased the land and closed it to the public for a decade. In 1945 it was finally reopened, but only for nonmotorized recreation.

This is backpacking country, and hikers can plan their walks on more than 20 well-maintained trails that crisscross and loop for about 75 miles. The area is drained primarily by the Cranberry River and the Middle Fork of the Williams River and their tributaries. Campers can dip their drinking water from the streams. The trails along the Cranberry River receive the most visitation since the river is stocked with trout, but many other trails provide serene walks into solitude. There are spectacular vistas from the high ridges, numerous water crossings in the valleys and more than a few steep climbs between the two.

A feeling of dampness often prevails in the region, for the Cranberry Back Country receives more rain and snow than the surrounding forest, and it is also more humid. Black flies and mosquitoes haunt hikers, even though the altitude is over 3500 feet. And, like parts of the tundra, it is wet just a few inches under the surface of the ground. This water table has some effect on the air temperature. The ground covering of sphagnum moss is always wet. An excellent insulator, the moss holds enough moisture to cool air above it, which is why hikers sometimes find frost on the ground in the summer months.

As rough as it appears, the entire Cranberry Back Country has an extremely fragile ecosystem. Great caution must be taken with fire; scars of a wildfire on Black Mountain in 1937 are still visible along one of the trails. With the continued protection it has been receiving, however, the Cranberry Back Country should remain as one of West Virginia's premier wild places.

HOW TO VISIT THE CRANBERRY BACK COUNTRY

The Cranberry Back Country is located within the Monongahela National Forest, north of White Sulphur Springs and a few miles east of Summit Lake. West Virginia Highways 39

One of the most unusual features of this area is Cranberry Glades, the state's largest highland bog covering approximately 400 acres. A short boardwalk leads visitors through an unusual plant community.   Photo by West Virginia Commerce Dept.

and 150 are the southern and western boundaries of this 53,000 acre wilderness region.

Like many West Virginia mountainous regions, the Cranberry Back Country is subject to drastic weather changes in short periods of time. Summer temperatures may average in the 70s but can drop into the 30s and 40s after a sudden storm. Winter temperatures may plunge as low as 20 degrees below zero. Be prepared for these changes by taking proper clothing when planning an extended stay in the area.

HIKING AND BACKPACKING: There are 75 miles of hiking trails in the wilderness, ranging from 2 to about 20 miles long. Many of the trails intersect, so a trip can be practically as long or as short as time and stamina allow. There are also many miles of old logging roads closed to vehicular traffic which, when combined with the trails, offer an even greater range of walking opportunities.

All trails are marked with blue paint blazes on trees, and intersections are signed. There are no bridges at stream crossings, and crossings are extremely difficult in high water conditions. On practically any trail you choose, expect plenty of uphill/downhill footwork, for the elevation in this region ranges from 2600 to 4600 feet, with steep valleys and forested ridges.

Backpackers will especially want to study the following topographic maps before starting out: Western Springs, SW and SE; Richwood; and Camden-on-Gauley — all West Virginia quadrangles. The area receives more than 60 inches of rainfall annually and nearly 100 inches of snow, so campers need to plan their trips carefully.

CAMPING: Camping is permitted anywhere in the Cranberry Back Country, but there are nine trail shelters available on a first-come, first-served basis. Each of these shelters has room for six campers and provides fireplaces and picnic tables. Camping permits are not required at this time, but this policy may change as visitation increases. Campers are advised to register at either the Cranberry Mountain Visitor Center or the Gauley Ranger Station before entering the region.

FISHING AND HUNTING: Hunting is permitted for grouse, turkey and deer in season.

Fishing draws many campers into the area, for all of the Cranberry River and part of the South Fork of the Cranberry are stocked with trout weekly in April and May and again in the fall. Anglers must have a valid West Virginia fishing license, trout stamp and a national forest stamp.

Additional hunting and fishing information is available from the Department of Natural Resources, 1800 Washington Street East, Charleston, WV 25305.

WILDLIFE OBSERVATION: Backpackers may see deer, turkey and possibly a black bear. This area has been officially designated as a sanctuary for black bear. Birders should be on the lookout for the hermit thrush, purple finch and Nashville warbler, for this is their southernmost breeding ground.

ADDITIONAL INFORMATION: A free brochure describing the Cranberry Back Country is available from the District Ranger, Monongahela National Forest, Richwood, WV 26261;

or from the Supervisor, Monongahela National Forest, Box 1548, Elkins, WV 26241. Backpackers should also plan to contact the West Virginia Highlands Conservancy, Box 711, Webster Springs, WV 26288, for their publications describing the region. One of the most helpful is their "Hiking Guide to the Monongahela National Forest."

The Cranberry River is stocked with trout, and backpacking trails along its banks receive heavy use from anglers during the fishing season. In winter, as shown here, only a few hardy backpackers visit the area.   Photo by West Virginia Commerce Dept.

DOLLY SODS
"Trekking through Tundra"

Dolly Sods is another of those unusual West Virginia wilderness areas filled with vegetation and terrain that really should not be there. At Dolly Sods the flora more closely approximates what is normally found much further north: wind-whipped spruce trees and a vast ground covering of peat and sphagnum moss. An unusual species growing here is sundew, a small insect-eating plant found among the rocks. Although the entire Dolly Sods region embraces over 30,000 acres, only 10,500 acres are set aside as wilderness; the remainder is in private ownership. This smaller tract, however, does provide backpackers and campers with most of the features characteristic of this complex ecological zone. There are hills and valleys, timber-covered ridges, open plains, great rocky outcroppings, numerous streams and waterfalls, boggy glades and even beaver ponds. The area is located on the Allegheny Plateau highlands, and as such receives fairly heavy rain and snowfall each year. Fog is a common occurrence as well and has led more than one hiker to become temporarily disoriented.

Dolly Sods was not always as bare of trees as it is now. A century ago this land was covered with dense stands of red spruce, hemlock and a variety of northern hardwoods, as was much of the Monongahela. Logging companies cut the timber with little thought for the future, and erosion left its mark. Without tree cover to hold the soil and water in place, flooding was frequent and actually drove a number of settlers from the area. One of the earliest families in the area was named Dahle, for which Dolly Sods is named. The local term *sods* refers to pastureland, for early pioneers used the land for grazing.

There are a number of theories of how the unusual boggy glades and associated plant life came to be growing in this part of West Virginia, and most involve the glacial activity that covered the area thousands of years ago. Seeds from more northern regions were frozen in the advancing ice, then deposited when the glaciers retreated. The plants found the conditions tolerable and have survived ever since.

Much of the wilderness is laced with small streams, and Red Creek, the major drainage of Dolly Sods, has a distinct dark coloration. This color is believed to be caused by tannic acid coming from sphagnum bogs and spruce needles, but with purification the water is safe to drink. There are numerous small waterfalls along many of the streams, and several trail crossings require wading.

One of the popular features of Dolly Sods is Bear Rocks, located just north of the actual wilderness boundary on Forest Service Road 75. This ridge is covered with an outcropping of massive white boulders that seem to have been dumped here as leftovers from some huge construction site. Much of Dolly Sods is rocky terrain, but not with the size of boulders found here.

The wilderness area was established by Congress in 1975, and since then the area has been under a wilderness-use permit system, even for day visitors. Nearly 30 miles of backpacking trails have been established by the U.S. Forest Service and various outdoor-oriented organizations, providing an excellent network of footpaths across the area.

The best time to visit Dolly Sods is probably during the summer and early fall. The open plains are filled with wild blueberries, and visitors come to fill their baskets with the tasty fruit. In September hawks can frequently be seen migrating southward across Dolly Sods. Later in the fall and throughout the winter temperatures drop, and as much as a foot of snow may fall during a single storm. The spring thaw does not usually occur until late April or May.

The first stop for any visitor to Dolly Sods should be at the Bell Knob fire tower, located north of the picnic ground on FS 75. Personnel in the tower can issue wilderness-use permits as well as provide information on latest trail conditions in the area. From the fire tower, continuing north along FS 75, it is a short distance to Red Creek campground and the short interpretive trail that introduces visitors to this unusual region.

Two backpackers return to civilization after spending several days in the Dolly Sods backcountry. There are numerous trails through the region leading across open plains, through spruce forests, beside beaver ponds and across streams.

HOW TO VISIT DOLLY SODS

The Dolly Sods Wilderness is located in the northern part of the Monongahela National Forest in portions of Tucker and Randolph counties, approximately 15 miles west of Petersburg and about 10 miles northeast of Laneville. To reach Dolly Sods, follow FS 19 east from Laneville for 5 miles, then north on FS 75 for 5 more miles. This route leads along the wilderness boundary and past several trailheads. It is also possible to reach Dolly Sods by driving north from Petersburg on W. Va. Highway 42, continuing approximately 3 miles beyond Maysville and turning south on FS 75.

HIKING AND BACKPACKING: There are nearly 30 miles of hiking trails in the wilderness, leading through both open and wooded terrain, beside beaver ponds, across streams and along old logging roads to provide a wide variety of hiking experiences. The longest single trail is just under 7 miles in length, but by connecting with other trails in the system much longer trips can be made.

Two good starting points for hiking are the Dolly Sods picnic ground on FS 19 and the Red Creek campground on FS 75 from which the Rohrbrough Plains and the Blackbird Knob trails lead, respectively. The Rohrbrough Plains Trail, three miles, leads across the more open plains of the region and provides a good look at the unusual landscape. This trail meets the Fisher Spring Run Trail, which can be followed back to FS 75 several miles above the picnic ground. Following the Fisher Spring Run Trail in the opposite direction leads to the Red Creek Trail, the major north-south trail in the wilderness.

At Red Creek campground, hikers can follow the Blackbird Knob Trail two miles to Blackbird Knob and there join the northern terminus of Red Creek Trail heading south across the wilderness. The Blackbird Knob Trail is interesting in that it meanders through both open terrain as well as spruce forest. It also has several creek crossings.

Various other trails lead off the Red Creek Trail, and backpackers planning to follow any of them should study two Forest Service maps of the wilderness that show these routes clearly. Each map measures an unwieldy 46 by 33 inches, with a scale of one-half inch to the mile. They are known as Secondary Base Series Maps, and cover the northern and southern halves of the wilderness. Each map is available for $.50 from the forest supervisor's office.

Wilderness-use permits are required for both day and overnight entry into Dolly Sods, and these may be obtained in advance from the district ranger offices in Elkins, Parsons, Richwood, Bartow, Marlinton, Petersburg or White Sulphur Springs. Open fires are permitted but not encouraged; portable stoves are preferred. Water is available from various streams but should be sterilized. Several primitive campsites have been established along the various trails for use by backpackers.

CAMPING: Camping in Dolly Sods is available at the Red Creek campground, located on FS 75 along the eastern wilderness boundary. There are approximately a dozen sites suitable for tents or self-contained recreational vehicles, and drinking water is provided.

Backcountry primitive campsites are located along the Breathed Mountain and Big Stonecoal trails but do not offer anything more than flat ground on which to pitch a tent. Camping is permitted throughout the wilderness but not within 100 feet of streams, trails or roads.

Additional camping is available nearby at Canaan Valley

In places Dolly Sods is similar to terrain found much further north, for it contains moss and lichens similar to those found in tundra regions. A number of unusual plants grow here, possibly brought down by advancing glaciers.

Photo by West Virginia Commerce Dept.

and Blackwater Falls state parks, as well as at various recreation areas in the Monongahela National Forest. For additional
information on camping in the state parks, write the Office of
Economic and Community Development, Travel Division,
Capitol Building, Charleston, WV 25305.

HUNTING AND FISHING: Both hunting and fishing are permitted throughout the Monongahela National Forest and in
Dolly Sods. Hunters may go after deer, bear and ruffed grouse
in season, while anglers try to meet the challenges offered by
both smallmouth bass and rainbow trout. The nearby Petersburg Fish Hatchery has developed an unusual golden trout
which has gained great favor among both resident and non-
resident anglers; it is simply a mutation of the rainbow, with an
overall yellow-gold coloration. Visitors can see these fish in the
Petersburg hatchery.
  For additional information, contact the Department of
Natural Resources, 1800 Washington Street East, Charleston,
WV 25305.

WILDLIFE OBSERVATION: Wildlife in the region includes
both deer and bear, but both are seldom seen by Dolly Sods
visitors. The best wildlife viewing is in early fall when several
species of hawks can be observed migrating southward over the
ridges.

RAFTING AND CANOEING: The streams within the actual
borders of Dolly Sods do not have enough water to provide for
white-water sports, but several rivers nearby do. One of the
most popular is the North Fork of the South Branch of the
Potomac River, beginning at Mouth of Seneca on W. Va. 28
and continuing downstream for about 15 miles.
  A list of white-water outfitters is available from the Office of
Economic and Community Development (see "Camping"
above).

ADDITIONAL INFORMATION: For additional information
on the Dolly Sods Wilderness and the Monongahela National
Forest, write the Monongahela National Forest, Box 1548,
Elkins, WV 26241. Information may also be obtained by
writing the West Virginia Highland Conservancy, Box 711,
Webster Springs, WV 26288.

WILDERNESS FOR THE FUTURE

Less than three centuries ago the entire North American continent was wilderness. Today only a small fraction remains, and in places its "wild" classification is questionable. No more wilderness can be created—only preserved—for future generations, but as often happens when technology and ecology meet, the future must be planned for now.

Americans have actually been working for wilderness preservation for many years. The designation in 1876 of Yellowstone as our first national park was but the first in a long series of steps since taken by presidential administrations, conservation-oriented organizations and dedicated individuals to protect the nation's wilderness heritage. When President Johnson signed into law the Wilderness Act of 1964 immediately designating 54 separate areas totaling 9.1 million acres to be preserved in their natural state, conservationists everywhere applauded. For this bill also directed various federal agencies to review additional areas for possible inclusion into the Wilderness System. Here, indeed, was a guarantee of wilderness for the future.

In compliance the U.S. Forest Service completed its first Roadless Area Review and Evaluation (RARE I) Program in 1973, suggesting various national forest tracts for wilderness designation. Two years later Congress passed the Eastern Wilderness Act, classifying 16 areas totaling 207,000 acres as wilderness. These were located in the South and East and include such popular sites as Caney Creek in Arkansas and West Virginia's Otter Creek. In the original 1964 act, only two Southern wild places received wilderness status: Linville Gorge and Shining Rock, both in North Carolina.

In 1977 the U.S. Forest Service began RARE II, another study of possible wilderness areas. Public interest was extremely

183

high and a total of 2919 such areas were inventoried in 38 states and in Puerto Rico. In the final Environmental Impact Statement released in early 1979, 624 of these areas were recommended for immediate wilderness status, and 314 areas were recommended for further study.

These "future study areas" will receive close scrutiny in the next few years, and many of them will probably receive wilderness designation by Congress. But what then? After these different areas have been classified, can there ever be any *additional* wild places to receive congressional protection?

The answer is yes. The prospects for future wilderness areas will never end.

By the year 1985 each national forest must have completed a comprehensive land and resource management plan, as directed by the National Forest Management Act of 1976. Certainly one of the alternatives for national forest use is as wilderness. This is particularly true in the South. Of the approximately 12.5 million acres of national forest land, only a small percentage is used by the logging industry to harvest timber, when compared to timber harvest from industry-owned or privately owned lands.

There is another way to have tracts designated and protected as wilderness, and that is by having a bill introduced into the legislature by any member of Congress. This is the most difficult path to follow because it takes the combined efforts and finances of many people over a long period of time. It does work, however, for public interest was largely responsible for establishment of Alabama's Sipsey Wilderness in Bankhead National Forest.

Not all future wilderness tracts must be in the national forests. The Wild and Scenic River System offers additional alternatives for enjoying the wilderness experience. These rivers need not provide the roller-coaster thrills of a Chattooga or Gauley River; indeed, the major requirements for inclusion into the system are just a lack of development along the riverbanks, and that the river be free flowing and without pollution.

Wilderness, of course, is many things to different people. Often it is as much a state of mind as it is a physical location. To a fisherman wilderness may be casting a fly to a rainbow trout, even though the car is parked just a few feet away. To the camper wilderness may be the fun of pitching a tent in a forest glen and cooking over a campfire, while a restaurant may be open just beyond the treeline.

Because of these differences, and because the congressional designation of a forest tract or river as wilderness means the end of all future development, there must be compromises between those who favor such restricted areas and those who oppose them. For some, such classification may mean the end of a job or the loss of property, and it must be remembered that not everyone is physically able to enjoy the rugged atmosphere a wilderness tries to preserve.

In a way, however, wilderness areas and wild places are like mountain summits. The top of the mountain, geographically, takes up very little space, but it is an extremely important space to mountain climbers. Man realized long ago the need to preserve wild areas, if for no other reason than to have a place to rekindle the human spirit, and that, today, more than anything else, is what wilderness is all about.

INDEX

WILD PLACES OF THE SOUTH

East Woods Press Books

Backcountry Cooking
J. Wayne Fears

The Fructose Cookbook
Minuha Cannon

The Healthy Trail Food Book
Dorcas Miller

Honky Tonkin'—A Travel Guide to American Music
Richard Wootton

Hosteling USA—The Official AYH Handbook

The Maine Coast—A Nature Lover's Guide
Dorcas Miller

The New England Guest House Book
Corinne Ross

Roxy's Ski Guide To New England
Roxy Rothafel

Sea Islands of the South
Bill & Diana Gleasner

Steppin' Out—A Guide to Live Music in Manhattan
Weil & Singer

Trout Fishing the Southern Appalachians
J. Wayne Fears

East Woods Pak-books™

Adirondack Rock and Ice Climbs
Thomas Rosecrans

Campfire Chillers
E.M. Freeman

Canoeing the Jersey Pine Barrens
Robert Parnes

Exploring Nova Scotia
Lance Feild

Hiking Cape Cod
Mitchell & Griswold

Hiking Virginia's National Forests
Karin Wuertz-Schaefer

Rocky Mountain National Park Hiking Trails
Kent & Donna Dannen

Tennessee Trails
Evan Means

Walks in the Catskills
Bennet & Masia

Walks in the Great Smokies
Rod & Priscilla Albright